QUILTS *in* BLOOM

QUILTS *in* BLOOM

A Garden of Inspiring Quilts and Techniques with Floral Designs

MARION HASLAM

CREATIVE PUBLISHING international

First published in the USA and Canada in 2004 by
Creative Publishing International, Inc.

18705 Lake Drive East
Chanhassen, MN 55317
1-800-328-3895
www.creativepub.com

President/CEO: Michael Eleftherio
Vice President/Publisher: Linda Ball
Vice President/Retail Sales: Kevin Haas
Executive Editor/Lifestyles: Alison Brown Cerier

First published in Great Britain in 2004
by Collins & Brown Limited
The Chrysalis Building
Bramley Road
London W10 6SP

The right of Marion Haslam to be identified as the author of this work has been asserted by her in accordance with the Copyright, Designs and Patents Act, 1988.

10 9 8 7 6 5 4 3 2 1

ISBN 1-58923-133-3

Photography by Jonathan Farmer and Thomas Skovsende
Designed by Lisa David
Project managed by Miranda Sessions
Copy-edited by Jane Read

Reproduction by Classicscan, Singapore
Printed and bound by Times Offset, Malaysia.

IMPORTANT
The author and publishers have made every effort to ensure that all instructions given in this book are safe and accurate. They cannot accept liability for any resulting injury or loss of damage to either property or person, whether direct or consequential and howsoever arising.

QUILT CREDITS
Front cover: *Almost Crewel* by Marilyn Badger
Page 1: *Grandma's Country Album II* by Claudine Hansen
Pages 2–3: *Tulips* by Edith Junglagen

CONTENTS

QUILTS AND FLOWERS

WHY ARE QUILTERS INSPIRED BY flowers? What is it about nature that provides quiltmakers with an endless source of inspiration? Flowers provide limitless color combinations for quiltmakers. Inspiration could grow from the dramatic contrast seen in the head of a tulip, as the lipstick red of the petals suddenly changes to white and then into inky black. The subtle striations in an iris petal which contain every possible tint and shade of violet and purple have inspired many artists.

Sometimes the sheer proximity of nature can awaken a creative urge, as American quiltmaker Emily Parson describes in the following extract from her website (www.emilyquilts.com).

*In the winter of 1997–98, my husband and
I bought our first house in the far suburbs of Chicago.
We had no idea of the beautiful gardens that were
lying dormant in our yard, waiting to surprise us.
The profusion of daffodils, crocus and tulips
that erupted in the spring renewed my enthusiasm for
my work. After ten years of living in the city,
I became reacquainted with the joys of having a
yard, flowers, birds and wildlife.*

Another reason for the popularity of flowers is that quilters are often avid gardeners. Both activities require hard work and involve tasks that are often broken into smaller parts, whether the person is weeding and pruning, or cutting fabrics, stitching, and building up blocks. Both require patience and a nurturing spirit not to mention creativity and a love of color, texture, and shape.

This love of flowers is a global affair—the American Quilter's Society has organized two contests in the past few years called "Flowers on Parade" and "My Garden". Many of the quilts and quiltmakers whose stunning work is shown in this book are also prizewinners at national and international shows.

HISTORICAL FLOWERS

This combined interest in floral quiltmaking and flowers in nature is not new. In the nineteenth century, floral quilt designs such as Whig Rose and Cockscomb were widely sewn. Botany, floriculture, and garden design were popular because they were seen as suitable accomplishments for ladies.

Botanical illustrations have been an important method of studying plants for centuries. Herbal drawings by sixteenth century artists and scholars were forerunners of important works of later centuries. A key figure, Swedish naturalist Carl Linnaeus, invented the modern classification and plant naming system first published in *Hortus Cliffortianus* in 1738. As a result of his work, botanical illustrators paid greater attention to scientific accuracy.

At the end of the eighteenth century, Pierre Joseph Redouté received royal patronage. French Empress Josephine Bonaparte was an avid gardener and rose lover. She commissioned Pierre Joseph Redouté to record plant varieties in a series of books. His subsequent work on roses, involving delicate details by stipple engraving, was published internationally. No wonder the rose became one of the most popular motifs in floral quiltmaking in the nineteenth century.

POPPY FIELD

Emily Parson
Illinois, USA
2001
82 × 82"
(208 × 208 cm)

This collage-style appliqué quilt features hand-dyed fabrics in a wide variety of tints and shades to reflect nature's limitless color palette. For Emily, poppies are one of the happiest types of flowers. She was inspired to make this quilt after many years of admiring the flowers in a neighbor's garden. The starting points for much of her recent work are her own photographs. This quilt was awarded first place for appliqué at the AQS Show, 2001.
American Quilter's Society

EXOTIC EXPLORATIONS

In the nineteenth century the public was captivated by the many expeditions taking place. In Britain, naturalist Sir Joseph Banks traveled on HMS *Endeavour* with Captain Cook, together with two artists. They journeyed around the world between 1868 and 1871 recording native plants as yet unknown in the rest of the world.

In North America, a great deal of the natural habitat of the country was unexplored as most of the population lived within fifty miles of the Atlantic coastline. When Thomas Jefferson became President he obtained government funding to finance the 1806 expedition to the Pacific Ocean by Lewis and Clark. Their findings were reported in the newspapers and as new plants were discovered, they surely captured the imaginations of quiltmakers back home.

In the second half of the nineteenth century, mail-order seed companies in England and America produced color catalogs featuring their many new plant varieties. This sparked a demand for exotic flowers and may have provided visual inspiration for quiltmakers looking for ideas.

During the early twentieth century floral inspiration could come from within the house. The Arts and Crafts style became popular, and artist William Morris designed a number of richly colored fabrics and wallpapers that featured floral and plant motifs.

**NORTH SHORE
BEAUTIES**

Jennifer Cooper
British Columbia,
Canada
2002
62 × 48"
(157 × 122 cm)

North Shore Beauties is
Jennifer's original design,
using Karen Stone's
New York Beauty
pattern. By playing with
the sizes of the blocks
on graph paper and a
photo-copying machine
she created this
multiblock quilt. The
sharp points in the
blocks use precise
foundation piecing
interspersed with filler
squares that create a
perpetual summer in
patchwork.

A few decades later in America, during the
Great Depression, homemakers were looking for
ways to make do. Quilting became a practical
way to turn fabric scraps into something beautiful and useful. Quilt patterns changed to
incorporate the small pieces. Styles varied from
folk-art quilts hastily sewn together to master-

pieces entered into national competitions offering
major prize money.

In the twentieth century, many quilters were
inspired by artists who depicted flowers in new
ways; Matisse, Van Gogh, Georgia O' Keefe, and
others left a permanent mark with their unique
floral styles in painting.

PARADISE IS A DAY IN THE GARDEN SHED
Irene MacWilliam
Belfast,
Northern Ireland
1989
38 × 39" (97 × 99 cm)

Irene's pictorial quilt is based on a newspaper obituary about a man who belonged to an upscale gardening club. After meetings he always insisted on walking home. What the other members did not realize was that he was living in the gardening shed. Machine appliqué and free machine writing was used for all the images, including the finely detailed borders of Oriental poppies and water lilies.

HOW TO USE THIS BOOK

Generations of quilters have created floral quilts designs, from early patchwork quilts of sunflowers and dahlias to the abstract designs of contemporary textile artists. This book plucks some of the finest examples of traditional and contemporary floral quilts and shares them with you in glorious color.

There are chapters about appliqué designs inspired by curved shapes of flowers and vines; block patterns that use geometric shapes to form floral motifs; quilting patterns based on flowers, leaves, and vines; bold floral borders to add to many kinds of quilts; and quilts embellished with embroidery, ribbon, and other textile arts. When a quilt uses more than one technique (say both appliqué and patchwork), it has been placed according to which technique is more prominent.

At the end of each chapter are step-by-step projects drawn from outstanding floral quilts. You can use these techniques in your own quilt designs. Note that projects have been placed according to the predominant technique in the entire original quilt and not necessarily the technique used in the project.

At the end of the book you will find templates for the projects, lists of official flowers, and resources for materials.

Enjoy walking in this quilted garden!

APPLIQUÉD QUILTS

In quiltmaking, appliqué is the technique of layering one fabric onto a background material. The top fabric can be cut to any shape and stitched in place by hand or machine. Because the appliqué motifs can be of any pattern or size, the technique is ideal for images such as flowers. The petals, leaves and stems can be round, oval, irregular, or entwining. The appliqué shapes can also be applied over larger motifs to build up layers—very useful for complex flower heads. Appliqué has been used in floral quilts for more than two hundred years. It is an extremely flexible method of pattern making.

IRIS QUILT

Unknown maker

c. 1930s

approximately 75½ × 83" (192 × 211 cm)

This 1930s quilt was a popular commercial design from the studio of professional quilt designer Ruby Short McKim. The flag irises are appliquéd onto a solid color background fabric in neat diagonal rows of rectangular blocks.

Collection of Patricia Cox Crews

BASKET BRODERIE PERSE

Maker unknown, USA
c. 1850
113 × 115"
(287 × 292 cm)

A central basket motif and three bouquets are surrounded by an appliquéd trellis and swag in a small red print. One of the three manufacturer's stamps visible on the backing fabric says "Lowell Bleachery Finish," a mill in Lowell, Massachusetts. University of Nebraska-Lincoln

QUEEN VICTORIA BRODERIE PERSE

Maker unknown
Dated 1843 and 1844
92½ × 109½"
(235 × 278 cm)
University of Nebraska-Lincoln

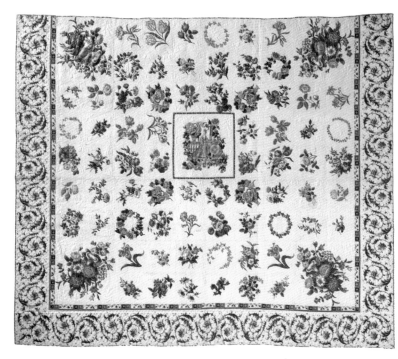

FLORAL APPLIQUÉ QUILTS OFTEN involve careful planning and consideration for the placement of motifs. Usually, the quiltmaker is doubling up on the fabric layers, unlike pieced patchwork where small pieces are sewn together with seams to form a single layer of cloth. This more spendthrift approach to quilt-making was criticized by quilt designer Ruby Short McKim in her 1931 book *One Hundred and One Patchwork Patterns*:

> *Appliqué is a form of patchwork more pretentious
> and extravagant than the good old-fashioned piecing
> variety. One layer of cloth, wholly for decoration,
> is applied to the background material with either
> blind or fancy stitching.*

TROPICAL GARDEN

Joanne Goldstein

Florida, USA

1998

50 × 51"

(127 × 130 cm)

Florida's lush landscaping, deep blue skies, and vibrant flora and fauna, all inspire Joanne's work. Her quilt captures this verdant and colorful world through a combination of piecing, broderie perse, silk ribbon embroidery, and bead and button embellishments. Look closely and you can see frogs, lizards, and birds camouflaged within the foliage.

Nevertheless, for floral quilts, appliqué is the more common technique. On historic American quilts dating from the 1800s to the 1860s, appliquéd flowers, urns, wreaths and vines are more common on East Coast quilts where quiltmakers had easier access to imported fabric and more time to spend on decorative quiltmaking. Quiltmakers who headed west on the pioneer trail were more likely to sew utilitarian patchwork block quilts.

Today, contemporary quiltmakers such as Debra Danko, Barbara McKie, and Emily Parson whose *Poppy Field* is shown on page 7, have moved floral appliqué onto an even higher artistic plane. Appliqué allows their ideas to be freely translated into cloth, whether they choose to produce abstract designs or photo-realism style quilts.

CHINTZ APPLIQUÉ (BRODERIE PERSE)

Traders have been importing Indian chintzes to Europe (and from Europe to the East Coast of America) since the seventeenth century. The glazed cotton fabrics featured elaborate patterns, including the tree of life, plant, bird, and butterfly designs, flower sprays, bouquets, baskets, and urns. Early Indian chintzes were block printed with dyes containing mordant, which meant that the colors were fast, unlike European printed cloth of the time. As early as 1643 the East India Company, major importers of this cloth to England, was suggesting design changes to their Indian manufacturers to increase the appeal of these exotic fabrics to their Western customers. Patterns became more elaborate, and Western flowers such as tulips, chrysanthemums, sweet peas, and hollyhocks were

CELEBRATION

Maureen Baker

Essex, England

1996

90 × 90"

(230 × 230 cm)

Self-taught using the book *Baltimore Beauties* by Elly Sienkiewicz, Maureen made this quilt over two years to celebrate her ruby wedding anniversary. The hand appliqué uses needle turn and reverse appliqué methods and the dahlia and rose buds in the bottom row are three-dimensional. Awarded first prize for intermediate quilts and second prize for decorative quilts at the National Patchwork Championships, UK, in 1996.

included alongside native Indian plants. Botanical accuracy was not a consideration—several different flower types would often be depicted growing on one stem and differences in scale were ignored.

In 1701, the importation of Indian chintzes was banned to protect wool and silk manufacturing in England. Similar embargoes also occurred in Britain's colonies and France. Because the supply of chintzes dried up, these ornate fabrics became even more expensive and highly prized. Affluent women stretched out the little fabric they could obtain by carefully cutting out the printed motifs and appliquéing them onto plain background cloth. This type of appliqué is known as cut-out or broderie perse (a French term, meaning

Persian embroidery). It is thought that these quilts were given this curious title because the quilt designs often imitated crewel embroidery. The term now generally refers to quilts with appliquéd chintz motifs. The trend for this style of quilt started in England in the late 1700s and spread to other countries.

As a result of the importation ban, manufacturers in Europe and textile centers such as Lowell, Massachusetts, began to design and print cloth in a similar style. The broderie perse style quilts were so popular that Western manufacturers designed "cheater" chintz fabrics, specifically for quiltmaking. As Jennifer Gilbert from the New England Quilt Museum explains:

These fabrics contained small motifs for the cut work, as well as large expanses of florals for use in quilt borders. Cotton fabrics for broderie perse appliqué became readily available after about 1840.

Individual floral motifs were appliquéd onto squares that were then sewn together as a patchwork with or without sashing. Alternatively, the pattern is built up in rings around a central motif. This frame or medallion format was most common in quilts from about 1775 to 1840. Finally, broderie perse can be combined with patchwork, the appliqué being used as a foil for the pieced design. Early broderie perse appliqués had a narrow turned edge and were attached using a fine buttonhole, feather, or slipstitch (blind stitch) in a neutral colored thread.

Today, suitable fabrics for appliqué are plentiful and available in any quilt shop in both large and small-scale patterns. Motifs from the natural world are still popular and can vary from realistic interpretations to cartoon-like designs in vibrant colors. As Joanne Goldstein (*Tropical Garden*, page 13) explains, flowers are a recurring theme in her quilting patterns:

The color and scent of beautiful flowers brings a sense of peace and serenity into my life. I enjoy

BALTIMORE ALBUM BRIDES QUILT
Wendy Lawson
London, England
2002
61½" × 63½"
(156 × 161 cm)

On September 11th 2001, Wendy was hand-sewing the final block on this quilt when news broke of the terrorist activity in America. The World Trade Center was later added to the floral wreath, and doves of peace were quilted in the outer borders.

BALTIMORE ALBUM

Maker unknown

Probably Maryland, USA

c. 1855

110 × 104"

(279 × 264 cm)

University of Nebraska-Lincoln

surrounding myself by my garden filled with wild flowers, potted plants and tropical, flowering trees. I am grateful to be able to wake up each morning to a garden that is always in bloom.

BALTIMORE ALBUM QUILTS

In the mid-nineteenth century, the East Coast city of Baltimore, Maryland, was a major port and the third largest city in the United States. One commodity that Baltimore imported was textiles, and the city also had a number of cotton mills. Three important factors—wealth and prosperity, a constant stream of people, and the availability of both locally produced and imported material—combined to set the stage for some of the most decorative and extraordinary quilts of this era, a style that has become known as Baltimore Album.

RR2K
Christine Thomas
and others
England, Scotland,
and Wales
1999–2000
54 × 44"
(137 × 112 cm)

The seven quilters who
were involved in this
millennium floral quilt
were spread across the
UK. The quilt was
designed by Christine
Thomas and each group
member— Christine,
Frances Birch, Sharon
Curtis, Sharon Lascelles,
Jane Marshall, Charlotte
Monckton and Sal
Spring—sewed a block
of 250 square inches.
Once all the blocks
were made, there were
250 square inches left
for putting the quilt
together.

Baltimore Album quilts are appliqué block quilts, often made by more than one person and featuring elaborate designs of flowers, fruits, urns, cornucopia, and occasionally patriotic and political motifs or commemorative patterns. They have bright colors offset by white or cream backgrounds. What makes them extraordinary is the complexity of the designs, and the technical proficiency of the women who sewed them.

Baltimore Album blocks also included hand-embroidered details such as stem tendrils and stamens. Many of the blocks featured inscriptions and dedications. The dates and signatures help quilt historians considerably in their research of nineteenth-century quilts. Baltimore Album quilt blocks occasionally recorded significant historical events in stitches, a tradition that continues to this day, as exemplified by the *Baltimore Album*

GRANDMA'S COUNTRY ALBUM II

Claudine Hansen

British Columbia, Canada

2000

73 × 70"

(185 × 178 cm)

Adapted from an original pattern by Robert Callaham in *McCall's Quilting Magazine*, this was a personal exercise in learning to appliqué. It's a goal Claudine certainly achieved—the American Beauty block (top, center) alone contains eighty-eight ¼-inch dots!

FLOWERS FOR FRIENDSHIP

Various makers

Avon, England

1975–1976

100 × 80"

(254 × 236 cm)

The American Museum in Britain

Brides quilt by British quilter Wendy Lawson (page 15).

Unlike the functional utility quilts sewn by American pioneers, Baltimore Album quilts were usually made by women with free time and money to spend on fabrics from Europe, India and Asia. Material was specially purchased for quiltmaking rather than using fabric scraps. The quilts were often sewn for commemorative or fund-raising purposes. They were also used to raise money for public buildings—churches, schools, hospitals and orphanages. This was done by "selling" the blocks to benefactors whose signatures were inked next to the appliqué designs. Whether sewn as gifts or for charities, it was likely that the blocks were sewn by several quiltmakers even if there was only one designer. The similar designs found in

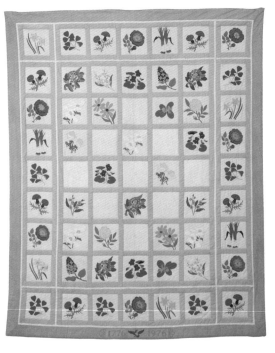

**COMPLIMENTS OF
THE SEASON**
Christine Reynolds
Kent, England
2002
39 × 39"
(100 × 100 cm)

The four seasonal panels
are bordered by rich
Hoffman fabrics and the
gold in the prints is
echoed in the metallic
thread of the machine
quilting. In each of the
panels the flowers and
leaves over-spill the
edges. The raw edges of
the appliqué are
covered with satin
stitching. French knots
delineate the leaf veins
and the flower heads of
the Rudbeckia blooms.

many of these quilts suggest that block patterns were available commercially.

The peak of popularity for this quilt style was in the 1840s and 1850s when quilts vied for splendor and precision. The ultimate goal for a Baltimore Album was as a bridal quilt. In this case the bedcover would have been kept for "best" and carefully stored when not in use. This accounts for the museum quality of these mid-nineteenth century quilts.

Since the latest quilt revival began in the 1970s (and particularly after the bicentennial celebrations in America), there has been a renewed fascination with this style of decorative quilt. Much of this interest is due to the work of quiltmaker and historian Elly Sienkiewicz who has researched traditional Baltimore appliqué patterns,

has written many books on the subject and runs an appliqué academy to pass on the patterns and technical skills shown by these quilts.

The more general term Album Quilt often refers to friendship or group quilts. Such quilts are an ideal showcase for floral patterns. Contemporary quiltmakers can create textile art that surpassed even their nineteenth-century predecessors because of the subtlety and diversity of fabrics now available. Fabric manufacturers are constantly launching new collections, and with such a demand for the latest designs, many fabrics only have one or two print runs. Quilt shops, mail-order suppliers and fat quarter subscription clubs all help fuel and satisfy the demand. The growth in Internet quilt companies also means that the latest fabric collections can be bought by quilters around the world.

SPIDER PLANT

Philippa Naylor

Dhahran, Saudi Arabia

2003

43 × 43"

(110 × 110 cm)

This striking, modern appliqué is a prime example of both technical expertise and a confident use of color. The central flower design features multi-lobed fantasy petals. Fusible adhesive (bonding agent) was used to appliqué the motifs, some of which are then edged in a close machine satin stitch. The four corners surrounding the central appliqué have trapunto quilted tendrils for extra definition.

One group's album quilt, *RR2K*, shown on page 17, was sewn by seven quilters in England, Scotland, and Wales to commemorate the millennium. Christine's hand-dyed fabric ties the blocks together and the dark green background causes the colors of the flowers to sparkle. This quilt shows a consistency in technical skill, that is not always apparent in collaboration quilts. Small details such as the hand-dyed cotton yarn used for the stamens and the variegated rayon thread in the zigzag stitching complement the hand-dyed fabric perfectly. Just as nineteenth-century quiltmakers took floral inspiration from many places, quilters today are equally open to novel sources for designs. The most unusual block in *RR2K* is the rhododendron block by Jane Marshall. Her source? A tattoo design on a sumo wrestler's bottom!

QUILT STYLES AND LAYOUTS

Traditionally, floral appliqué quilts have followed a number of formats—album style in which blocks, usually of the same size, use a variety of patterns; repeating blocks separated by solid color squares or sashing strips; frame (medallion) style in which a central design is surrounded by a number of pieced borders or appliqué flower sprays; and finally the four-block format. Quilt dealer Terry Clothier Thompson noticed this four-block quilt

FLOWER BASKETS

Maker unknown
Probably Ohio, USA
c. 1925
86½ × 78¾"
(220 × 200 cm)

This unusual quilt is
made from crocheted
baskets appliquéd onto
a cotton backing.
Variegated threads give
further interest to the
baskets, which are filled
with embroidered
flowers. A vine of
full-blown red roses
entwines around the
border, and diamond
cross-hatch quilting
completes the quilt. The
bright pastel color
scheme is typical of the
1920s and 1930s.
University of Nebraska-
Lincoln

regularly cropped up during a quilt documenta-
tion program in Kansas between 1986 and 1989
and she named it "appliqué by the yard." Such
appliqué quilts dated from the nineteenth century
and each featured four 36-inch (91½-cm) square
blocks. Because of the large scale of the blocks,
these appliqué designs were fast to hand-sew. The
central designs would often be surrounded by a
complementary pattern such as vines, baskets, or a
simple pieced sawtooth border. A skilled quilt
designer can devise a pattern in which elements
from one block link visually with the next block,
either through the motifs physically touching or
through symmetry and mirror-imaging. This leads

to secondary patterns being formed and disap-
pearance of divisions between individual blocks.
Look at the *Tulips and Roses* quilt on page 48 for a
fine example of this visual dexterity.

Contemporary quiltmakers work with bolder
formats to suit their photo-realism style of quilts
(see pages 33 and 35). Another format option is
to have a single main image in the quilt, such
as *The Spider Plant* by Philippa Naylor on
page 20. Modern-day quilts also continue the
traditions of the Baltimore Album quilts as shown
by *Flowers for Friendship*, a quilt made by
staff at the American Museum in Britain to mark
the Bicentennial in 1976. The quilt includes

symbols for the British Isles as well as many emblem flowers for US states such as the black-eyed Susan for Maryland. Unlike Baltimore Album quilts in which each appliqué block is different, this modern friendship quilt repeats images and also mirror-images some flowers. This has enabled the quilt's designer, Barbara Meru Frears, to achieve a pleasing balance of colors and imagery.

BASKET QUILTS

Baskets—new ones, old ones, perfectly gorgeous ones, absolutely original ones—all a joy to behold.

Carrie Hall's and Rose Kretsinger's obvious enthusiasm for basket quilts was thus expressed in their book *The Romance of the Patchwork Quilt*, published in 1935. However, basket quilts are not a twentieth-century phenomenon. A century ear-

GRANDFATHER'S NOT GRANDMOTHER'S GARDEN

Margaret Tashiro Caccamo
New York, USA
2001
104 × 85"
(264 × 216 cm)

Margaret's delightful quilt deservedly won a host of awards at quilt shows in 2002 and features a wealth of details. The pieced basket method was learned at an Eleanor Burns workshop. The realistic flowers in the baskets and borders use techniques such as appliqué, ruching, and beading.
Quilters Newsletter Magazine

lier, quiltmakers were also discovering the delights of combining patchwork and appliqué in the same block, as baskets are a natural companion to flower blocks. And like many patchwork blocks, the same basket pattern sometimes developed independently in different states or countries.

Unlike the Amish quiltmakers of Lancaster County, Pennsylvania, who made basket quilts in strong, plain colors, other quilters used the patch-work blocks as starting points for embellishment with appliquéd plants, blooms, and decorative handles. Many of the pieced blocks are based on triangles, squares, and diamonds. In the quilt shown on page 21, crochet and embroidery replace piecing.

Basket quilts provide a good opportunity for quiltmakers to express their individuality when sewing a group quilt, never exhibited more clearly

FLOWERS FOR ISOBEL
Members of
The Quilters' Guild
New South Wales,
Australia
1999–2001
97 × 84"
(247 × 213 cm)

Members contributed the blocks, and the quilt top was assembled by Chrissy Sheed. The variety of flowers and colors makes this a lively quilt. Some blocks are signed by their makers. The hand quilting is a combination of echo quilting and floral and leaf designs in the triangles and border. This quilt won the Judges' Commendation Award, Sydney Quilt Show, 2001.

than in the quilt, *Flowers for Isobel* as shown on page 23, which was made for Isobel Lancashire on her retirement as president of the Quilters' Guild of New South Wales, Australia. Each of the 67 blocks sewn by members of the Guild contained a unique two-colored, pieced basket. However, it is the variety of the floral contents of each basket that astounds. There are broderie perse blooms, three-dimensional flowers created from yo-yos (Suffolk Puff patchwork), and folded and manipulated flower heads. The boldest three-dimensional flower is the sunflower sixth row from the bottom, far right. This over-sized bloom is comfortably at odds with the scale of its container. The quilt also features traditional needleturn appliqué and pieced kaleidoscope flowers (fourth row from top-far left).

Floral designs give quilters the flexibility to

VINES WITH BIRDS AND FLOWERS
Maker unknown
Ohio, USA
c. 1950
93 × 76½"
(236 × 195 cm)

This kit quilt features an unusual pattern that has been carefully designed to fit the contours of a bed. To save time (and fabric) the "second row" is blank because it would have been folded under a pillow. Although this quilt was sewn in the 1950s, the pattern probably dates from at least a decade earlier. University of Nebraska-Lincoln

incorporate a host of garden-inspired images, as shown in Margaret Tashiro Caccamo's *Grandfather's not Grandmother's Garden,* (page 22). The Grandmother's Flower Garden design is a classic pieced hexagon pattern (page 54) and this quilt's intriguing title is a reference to Margaret's father-in-law, whose magnificent garden provided the ideas for the flower types included in her quilt. Other garden-inspired details are diamond lattice setting strips reminiscent of brick pathways in both formal and kitchen gardens and the half-circle edging design common to both Japanese gardens and many municipal parks. (More basket quilts are shown on pages 56 and 57)

TWENTIETH-CENTURY QUILTS

In America during the 1920s, the Colonial Revival movement encouraged quilters to celebrate and

MILLIE'S QUILT

Millie Chaput
Minnesota, USA
c. 1920
70 × 85"
(178 × 216 cm)

Despite the simple flower design, quiltmaker Millie Chaput has carefully arranged the blocks to create a secondary pattern through the mirror-imaging effect of the leaves. A wide variety of everyday dressmaking cottons in spots, plaids, and small prints are typical of the decade and add spirit to the design.
Collection of Patricia Cox Crews

**WHERE HAVE ALL
THE FLOWERS GONE?**

Norma Bassett
Massachusetts, USA
1996
72 × 51"
(183 × 130 cm)

This dramatic botanical
quilt has great personal
significance. It was
started as a tribute after
the deaths of Norma's
husband and a favorite
quilting teacher. The
amaryllis design is taken
from a Christmas card
published by the
Metropolitan Museum
of Art in New York. The
panel layout creates the
illusion of a balanced
design, although the
actual pattern is not
symmetrical. The subtle
tonal variation within
the limited color palette
results in a stunning
quilt.

rekindle their colonial past. As quilts embody the creativity and artistry of the "common people," there was a rush to both reproduce traditional patterns and design new ones. Marie Webster was a well-known pattern designer across the United States. Although she did not make her first appliqué quilt until 1909 when she was 50 years old, in 1911 she presented pastel, floral appliqué

LITTLE BROWN BIRD
Margaret Docherty
Durham, England
1994–1997
84 × 84½"
(213 × 215 cm)

The 8" (20 cm)
Baltimore Album style
appliqué blocks are
arranged in groups of
four with related styles
or colors. Blocks are set
on point so wreaths
make good use of the
block space. The outer
borders, especially the
corners, are superb
examples of balanced
design and accurate
spacing.
American Quilter's
Society

quilts in *Ladies' Home Journal*. Within two years the magazine printed 14 of Marie Webster's mainly floral patterns in full color, thus kick-starting the twentieth-century quilt revival. In the 1920s and 1930s Marie sold patterns and stamped quilt tops through advertisements, the latter at a cost of between $8 and $12.

In the 1920s Rose Kretsinger, author of *The Romance of the Patchwork Quilt in America* with Carrie Hall, sewed and reproduced old quilt designs as part of the Colonial Revival movement. One such pattern, *Oriental Poppy*, featured in her book, was adapted from a late-nineteenth-century quilt. The bold, stylized design uses a nine-block format. The two-color appliqué

SUNFLOWER QUILT
Caroline (Carrie)
Carpenter
Vermont, USA
1870–1890
84 × 78"
(213 × 198 cm)

Although its design
suggests the bold, floral
patterns of the 1970s,
this quilt was actually
sewn a century earlier.
Shelburne Museum

**CACTUS AND
COCKSCOMB**

Maker unknown
Probably Ohio, USA
1858
84 × 84"
(213 × 213 cm)
Collection of Patricia
Cox Crews

**CROWNED WITH
GLORY—RIGHT
ROYALLY**

Zena Thorpe
California, USA
1996
89 × 86"
(226 × 218 cm)

Zena was inspired to
sew this quilt after a visit
to the House of Lords
in London where she
saw rich embroideries,
carpets and furniture.
Nine crowns and
coronets are entwined
by blooms in this
Jacobean-style quilt.
Winner of the Founders
Award at the
International Quilt
Festival, USA, 1996.
International Quilters
Association

poppy blocks are separated by a sawtooth sashing and edged by a scalloped border and more poppies. The pattern was sold through the national magazines, *Farm Journal and Farmer's Wife,* for 10 cents. Such national exposure meant that these published patterns were reproduced on a large scale. Rose's own quilts were much fancier. One example, *Paradise Garden,* finished in 1946, was a complex adaptation of a prizewinning quilt by a professional pattern designer, Pine Hawkes Eisfeller. Rose may have been spurred on to sew *Paradise Garden* because Pine's quilt won the top prize in a national quilt contest in 1942, while her own placed second!

BOTANICAL ART FLOWER

Noriko Haba

Nara, Japan

1997

71 × 59"

(180 × 150 cm)

This quilt includes the cherry blossom and chrysanthemum, national flowers of Japan, as well as other flowers that have been selected as official flowers. A variety of techniques are used to interpret the blooms including foundation piecing and fine hand appliqué. In the two blocks at the top Noriko has cleverly selected patterned and textured fabrics to depict the roses and leaves for a naturalistic effect.

One of the most prolific quilt designers of the twentieth century was Ruby McKim, whose syndicated columns appeared weekly in many American newspapers. Her floral patterns, such as Pansy, Tulip and The Trumpet Vine, were compiled into a bestselling book, *One Hundred and One Patchwork Patterns*. They clearly reflected the Art Deco mood that was sweeping the design world between the two World Wars. McKim often took a single flower such as an iris or poppy and designed each as appliqué patterns and stylized geometric blocks that could be pieced with straight lines. During the 1920s and 30s, many commercial patterns for floral quilts were available and featured cheerful appliquéd flowers, such as nasturtiums, dandelions, and pansies. The Stearns & Foster company,

FLORAL ALBUM

Maker unknown

Possibly Pennsylvania, USA

c. 1920

87 × 86"

(220 × 218 cm)

This album quilt is filled with symbolism, from the black silk used as a background fabric, to the crucifix in the second row, to the choice of flowers themselves—marigolds for grief and despair, primroses for childhood and anemones for the winter of life. Some of the flower petals have extra stuffing for definition, and small embroidered sprigs are stitched between. University of Nebraska-Lincoln

manufacturers of "Mountain Mist" batting (wadding), used the packaging on their products to feature patterns, including designs for hollyhocks and sweet peas. The flour and animal foodstuffs manufacturers went one stage further. Not only did their labels feature patchwork and appliqué blocks, but the sacks themselves were made of cotton printed in brightly colored prints, ideal for recycling into quilts when money was tight.

The majority of floral quilt kits featured one of three design formats. First, if the fabric was supplied in a mail-order kit, the background cloth would have stamped motifs to be covered by the appliqué shapes. Such blocks were repeated four,

nine, or twelve times. Second, the patterns could be of the same style as a Baltimore Album, featuring different block patterns. Third, layouts with medallion centers, possibly of a bouquet or an elaborate wreath, would be surrounded by one or two leaf and flower vine borders. This latter design was particularly popular during the 1930s when designs were adapted to a rectangular format to suit the fashion for twin beds.

FINE APPLIQUÉ

Over the years different flowers have taken on important meanings and symbolism. In the eighteenth century, books were published defining the secret meaning of flowers, and in 1819, a

French publication *Le Language de Fleurs* was vital for paramours wanting to choose flowers with a hidden message. For example, posies of gypsophila (baby's breath) symbolize everlasting love, purple violets mean "you occupy my thoughts," and yellow tulips denote hopeless love. Other flowers have more open meanings, such as the cherry blossom, known in Japanese as *Sakura*. Although not native to Japan, the cherry blossom was adopted as a national flower. It is an important symbol of the arrival of spring and represents spiritual beauty. Noriko Haba's quilt, *Botanical Art Flower*, celebrates such national symbolism through the types of flowers she has chosen.

In the nineteenth century, the hidden meanings of flowers were incorporated into quilt designs, especially bridal quilts or album quilts. These often commemorated the departure from home of a family member. Such associations can be equally as effective for contemporary makers in order to give a variety of meanings to a quilt. The work of Australian quilter Julie Haddrick (see *Spirit of my Place* on page 43) illustrates how a quilt can have several emotional 'as well as practical layers. Her large machine-pieced pictorial landscape contains many details that have a personal symbolism for past, present, and future. For example, an appliquéd dove signifies the Holy Spirit, sustaining life and regeneration.

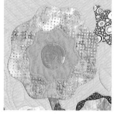

WHIGGED OUT ON THE WEST COAST
Andrea Perejda
California, USA
2002
75 × 75"
(191 × 191 cm)

Using traditional Whig Rose and Rose of Sharon patterns, this quilt dramatizes fresh colors. Hand appliquéd and quilted, it won five awards for color, appliqué and quilting in 2001 and 2002, including second place for innovative appliqué at the International Quilt Festival, USA. Quilters Newsletter Magazine

**IN REMEMBRANCE
OF NANNY**

Nancy Rink

California, USA

2002

76 × 72"

(193 × 183 cm)

As a child Nancy slept
under quilts sewn by
her great-grandmother.
This inspired her to sew
this folkloric design in
remembrance of a
favorite quilt. The
brightly patterned
appliquéd urns and
vases were inspired by
Spanish pottery, drawing
on Nancy's heritage. This
quilt was a finalist in
*QNM's Quilts: Reflections
of Heritage* competition,
2000.

Quilters Newsletter
Magazine

For centuries, quilts have been used as memorials to loved ones who have died. The stitching of memorial quilts can comfort the quiltmaker and the floral symbolism can provide a clear message of love, loss, and grief. The appliqué and embroidered album quilt by an unknown Philadelphia quiltmaker (on page 30) is an excellent example of this type of stitchery and provides subtle clues to interpret the symbolism.

In the twenty-first century, when time is often the primary consideration, quiltmaking continues to offer a counterbalance to a rush mentality. While techniques such as fused (bonded) appliqué offer an alternative to time-consuming hand stitching, for many quiltmakers the desire to create hand-crafted heirlooms often overrides the pressure to sew against the clock. Two masters of contemporary quiltmaking who exemplify these traditional skills are Zena Thorpe and Margaret Docherty, whose prizewinning quilts have become classics. For example, Margaret's quilt, *Little Brown Bird*, has won a total of four major awards including the Best in Show at the National Patchwork Championships in the UK (1997), C&T Publishing Baltimore Album Revival (1998) and the International Quilt

**SUMMER
SYMPHONY**
Emily Parson
Illinois, USA
2001
42 × 44"
(107 × 112 cm)

Emily uses the day lily as
her subject matter, a
common flower in
Illinois gardens during
the summer. She
manages to capture the
varied tones in the
petals by using an
assortment of hand-
dyed fabrics. The quilt
has a feeling of great
movement, achieved by
angling the five blooms
and the leaves as if they
are gently swaying in a
light breeze.
Charles Art and Music
Festival collection

Association, Houston (1999). The quilt took Margaret two and a half years to complete. Fine hand appliqué and hand quilting draws on the skills of past generations of needlewomen. By using a vast selection of patterned fabrics available today on a commercial tea-dyed background fabric, Margaret created a modern heirloom.

Zena Thorpe lives in the USA but visits to her native England and English decorative arts often inspire her lavish quilts. Skilled draftsmanship enables her to produce complex designs that require about a year and a half to complete. Half the time is spent on the hand appliqué and the remainder on the quilting. Her quilts have an energy coming from the variety of colors and fabrics. For example, *Crowned with Glory—Right Royally* (page 28) contains printed cottons, damask, and lamé materials with metallic and gold lamé thread adding richness.

BRIGHT BLOOMS

Just as during the Colonial Revival in the 1920s quiltmakers today often pay reference to earlier quilt styles, imagery, and techniques. All the main textile manufacturers are now printing cottons using archived patterns from museums or quilters' fabric collections. The popularity of such heritage collections indicates that there is a healthy demand for replica quilts based on traditional designs. However, another group of quiltmakers takes cues and ideas from earlier quilts and revitalizes the designs with unique fabric, technique, or some other twist.

Yvonne Porcella, a California quilt artist, well-known for her brightly colored quilts, openly

CRIMSON DELIGHT
Yvonne Porcella
California, USA
1998
42¾ × 58"
(109 × 147 cm)

Machine appliqué is used to great effect in this piece typical of Yvonne's exuberant quilt style. The brightly colored flowers and leaves are given further definition by the contrasting satin stitching around the appliqué. All the motifs are free cut, and careful choice of hand dyed fabrics provides a subtlety to the bright, modern color scheme, which is hand-and machine quilted. Although the border design is made in four separate panels, the illusion is of one flowing vine.

acknowledges use of traditional designs. Her quilt *Crimson Delight* (page 34) was inspired by nineteenth-century quilts with their urns of flowers and vine borders. However, by enlarging the central urn motif to fill the central panel and by her exuberant use of color, the resulting quilt is definitely a creation of the twentieth century.

The flower most often reinterpreted in quilts over the centuries is probably the rose. Roses were cultivated by the Chinese 500 years before the birth of Christ. They have inspired quiltmakers for two centuries but were especially popular in the middle of the nineteenth century when the red, white and green quilt was at its zenith. One frequently used appliqué rose design was the Whig Rose (Democrat Rose) which was popular until about 1870. The two names refer to the main political parties which were in power and opposition at the time in America. The Whig Party represented the common man and was in power for two decades. Although it suffered defeat in the 1852 election and disappeared from the American political

scene, it is immortalized in several political appliqué blocks, including Whig's Defeat and the Whig Rose. Traditional interpretations of this quilt are shown on pages 94 and 114. Compare this to Andrea Perejda's modern version on page 31. The positioning of the individual appliqué pieces in each of the five blocks is similar to the original, but the offset corner arrangement of the blocks gives a fresh twist to this well-known pattern.

Another rose design that quiltmakers have often interpreted is the Rose of Sharon. The design features a large, central flower from which rose buds and leaf stems radiate. This popular pattern takes its name from the Song of Solomon in the Bible's Old Testament:

I am a rose of Sharon, a lily of the valley.
As a lily among brambles, so is my love among maidens.

Quilt displays at agricultural shows throughout the nineteenth century allowed such fashionable appliqué patterns to be seen by many. This exposure fueled their popularity as other quiltmakers copied or adapted the patterns, depending on their own skills and the availability of fabric. Many of the rose quilts from this era featured red and green cloth, a popular combination used with white. Variable fading often occurs in these quilts. It happens because the red dye, (often called Turkey Red although the dye color originated from India), is a fast dye resistant to fading. In contrast, the green fabric used a dye called Fugitive Green. Over the years, the blue component has faded evenly from the green fabric, leaving a soft tan color, whereas the red remains bright.

FLOWERS AND VIEW

Sue Wademan
Queenstown,
New Zealand
2003
17 × 12"
(42 × 30 cm)

Tiger lilies are one of Sue's favorite flowers. A vase of blooms on her balcony overlooking Lake Wakatipu inspired this collage. Dyed and printed cottons are combined with sheer fabrics to create an image of riotous color. Oil pastel was added to the petals for extra shading. Machine quilting with rayon and metallic threads was used to complete the quilt.

CHRYSANTHEMUM

Bethan Ash

Cardiff, Wales

2000

57 × 57"

(145 × 145 cm)

Large-scale contemporary wall quilts can be as effective as modern art paintings. Machine pieced, appliquéd, and quilted using commercially dyed cottons, this was made when Bethan was having a break from working with bright colors. She finds that periods spent concentrating on muted or one-color quilts helps her to find greater meaning when she returns to color. Abstractions and spacial relationships are an important part of her work. This composition needs no embellishment to the spare design.

RAW EDGE APPLIQUÉ AND COLLAGE QUILTS

Today, many quiltmakers use a medium of collage-style appliqué to create pictorial wall quilts. The oversized flowers have the same impact as hyper-realism paintings, such as those by Georgia O'Keefe. Well-known quilt artists working in this way include Debra Danko, Emily Parson, Barbara McKie, and Deb Schwartzman. Hand-dyed and painted fabrics are an integral part of collage quiltmaking because the subtle colors are sympathetic to the subject matter.

Unlike traditional floral appliqué in which all pattern pieces are planned and cut at the start, the elements of collage quilts are built up slowly. Raw edge appliqué is a technical term used to describe the collage method that has gained popularity with the advent of iron-on fusible bonding tape. These non woven materials act like an adhesive, gluing appliqué shapes onto a background fabric. Their widespread availability since the late 1980s has encouraged quilters to experiment with collage-style designs. Because the fusible adhesive (bonding agent) tends to make the appliquéd fabric slightly stiff, it can be easy to use and makes the finished textiles particularly suitable as wall quilts. This technique enables quilt artists to act in an intuitive way, building up fabric collages in layers. Australian artist Sue Wademan (page 35) uses a variety of fabrics depending on the effect required. Base layers are

INDIAN DAISY

Ingrid Press

East Sussex, England

2002

31 × 22"

(79 × 56 cm)

Ingrid used hand-dyed and commercial fabrics in a joyful palette of colors for this small quilt. The large flower appliqués were sewn from the back. The raw edges were oversewn with a decorative looped machine stitch. Simple piecing provides a canvas for a great deal of machine and hand quilting. The daisy motifs are machine quilted, and their flower heads are emphasized by appliqués or small beads.

usually bonded to the background and oversewn before subsequent layers are added on top.

Unlike traditional appliqué in which templates are used for accurate cutting and fitting together, many quiltmakers cut freely into the fabric without following any patterns. Study of printed illustrations, careful observation of flowers, sketching, and photography are necessary in order to be familiar with the shape and curvature of the petals and leaves. Edith Jungslagen's *Tulips* quilt on page 39 shows how careful study of the color striations within the flower can be repli-

DAISY DAISY

Mary Mayne

Hertfordshire, England

2000

24 × 24"

(60 × 60 cm)

Inspired by the old love song, "Daisy Daisy—give me your answer do!," the petals are appliquéd onto a strip-pieced background and secured with straight line machine stitching. Mary's clever use of a wide variety of subtle white-on-white and grey print fabrics gives the flowers great depth.

Winner of the Sue Ridgewell Challenge Trophy awarded by the Quilters' Guild of the British Isles in 2000 this piece inspired a larger quilt (60 × 84" or 152 × 213 cm) which is now in a private collection.

cated with a high degree of accuracy in hand dyed fabrics for a realistic portrait. Large cartoons (drawings) at the same scale as the finished work can also be used as a plan for the correct placement of fabrics, or it can be done instinctively, usually with photographs or magazine tear sheets as initial inspiration for petal shapes. Colors from the quilter's fabric stash are auditioned for suitability. Parts of the collage are built up gradually, using a design wall. The method of appliqué uses a fusible adhesive (bonding agent) and the edges of the motifs are not turned under. The fabric is cut to size, and the various layers are ironed onto a background fabric. Some quilters stitch around the raw edges, using a machine satin stitch or blanket stitch. In other cases the fused pieces are

held down by dense all- over quilting, usually by machine, because the fusing makes hand quilting through the various layers more difficult. Decorative stitching is often used at the quilting stage to secure the fabrics if the quilts are to be laundered.

Like any new technique, individual quiltmakers adapt the design process to suit their own preferences or facilities within their sewing spaces. Well-known American quilt artist Caryl Bryer Fallert has completed a number of stunning floral quilts with large macro images of flowers. She uses photographs simplified into line drawings which she scans into her computer. She can then experiment with various color layouts and combinations. The line drawing is enlarged (onto paper attached to a wall) using an overhead projector, and templates for the individual appliqué pieces are cut out. As she explains, this approach enables her "to capture the beauty and energy of the blossom without making a photorealistic reproduction."

HAWAIIAN QUILTS

Anthurium, orchids, hibiscus, and gladioli all bloom in profusion on this tropical American state and the Big Island of Hawaii is the center of orchid growing in the world. The tropical colors and bold shapes of the indigenous flowers and plants have nurtured a specific style of appliqué since the late nineteenth century. Hawaiian quilting also clearly reflects the importance of cross-cultural influences in evolving a new quilt style. For years the islanders had exposure to many foreign visitors, from Captain Cook in 1778 to whalers, explorers and merchants from Russia, Europe, and the Orient. However, the major influence on their stitching traditions is credited to New England missionaries, who arrived in 1820, bringing with them traditions of fine American needlework and examples of quilts. The islanders already stitched with implements made from bone, worked on tree bark cloth called *tapa*, and printed with natural dyes. However, the missionaries brought metal needles that enabled the island women to sew finer stitches. The Hawaiian women incorporated the same designs on the quilts that they had used in their earlier printing. It is thought that their designs were also influenced by the cut paper designs known as *Scherenschnitte* and brought by German missionaries in the 1860s.

TULIPS
Edith Jungslagen
The Netherlands
2000
67 × 94" (170 × 240 cm)

Machine appliquéd and quilted, this quilt is truly impressive. Each flower head is about 40" (102 cm) tall.

WRAGG TIME

Mary Mayne

Hertfordshire, England

1997–1998

84 × 84"

(213 × 213 cm)

This quilt was originally a card design by Esther Wragg and reproduced with the artist's permission. Mary enlarged the original design into this large quilt pattern. The nine background squares contain grids, stripes, spots, and swirls and are decorated with fantasy flowers in bonded appliqué, freezer paper appliqué, and machine piecing. The elaborate hand quilting is different in each section and adds to the exuberance of the modern design.

Hawaiian appliqués have a unique style. They are usually composed of a symmetrical central motif that is hand sewn with a running stitch to a plain background cloth called *kahua*. Traditionally, only two fabrics are used, a lighter cloth for the background and a darker or more vibrant color for the appliqué. The central motif *ho'olau* is cut from one single piece of fabric, requiring dextrous fingers and confident cutting skills. To create the repeating, radiating image, a large fabric square is first folded three times to produce a triangle of fabric that is an eighth of the whole. The design is drawn freehand onto the triangle (although paper and cloth patterns have also been used), and then the pattern outline is cut with scissors. When unfolded, the Hawaiian pattern opens out to create a joined-up pattern of leaves, stems, and flowers, much like a garland of paper dolls.

As these motifs can measure up to 120 inches (305 cm) square, the original patterns can be extremely complex creating curvilinear patterns with branching secondary designs. The motif is then pinned to the backing fabric and, in traditional quilts, hand appliquéd. The central design can be surrounded by a decorative border, called a *lei* after the

floral garland. The border can be cut separately or attached to the main design and cut as one piece. The quilt top is layered with batting (wadding) and a backing fabric and the contour (echo) quilting starts near to the center. The lines of hand quilting usually follow the shape of the central motif and continue until the edges of the quilt top are reached. In Hawai this style of quilting is known as *kuiki lau* and is normally done in white thread. In modern Hawaiian quilts, the patterns are often adapted to a smaller block format rather than a single

HAWAIIAN DAFFODIL
Edyth Henry
Hampshire, England
1996
39 × 39"
(100 × 100 cm)

Edyth's appliqué shows a spring flower common to many European and North American gardens. This elegant design is sewn as a tablecloth, and is mostly unquilted. Most of Edyth's designs are quilted using a contour line every half inch (1⅓ cm). (See the English Daffodil on page 88 for another interpretation of this design.)

QUEEN KAPIOLANI'S FAN
Unknown maker
Hawaii, USA
Twentieth century
83 × 75"
(211 × 191 cm)

The appliqué pattern is named after one of the last members of the Hawaiian royal family. The four small, central fans are a variation on the cockscomb flower. The American Museum in Britain

HIBISCUS

Isobel Lancashire
New South Wales,
Australia
1995
35 × 36" (88 × 92 cm)

Designed for Isobel by fellow Australian quiltmaker Judy Hooworth, this exuberant hand-appliquéd quilt captures the lushness and vitality of traditional Tivaevae work, although this piece is densely hand-quilted. The bold petal-shaped border provides a colorful counter-balance to the central motifs.

large motif. This makes it easier to appliqué the patterns to the background. There is now greater freedom to use a wider variety of fabrics. Hawaiian-born quiltmaker Kathy Nakajima of Japan is typical of this new generation. She uses hand-dyed fabrics and batiks for both the appliqué and background. These mottled fabrics provide a random element to the formal designs.

Islanders take inspiration from native flowers and plants, such as the frangipani (*plumeria*) lily of the valley (*lilia O ka awawa*),breadfruit (*ulu*), and mango. Many superstitions surround Hawaiian appliqués, although their authenticity can only really be confirmed by the islanders. It is said that the breadfruit pattern is the first

design a quilter tackles because it it ensures that many more quilts will follow. Making quilts as a gift is seen as the greatest expression of love, and the quilter would normally sleep under her completed quilt for one night before giving it away. When the appliqué design is of flowers or foliage, only one type of plant is used for the pattern because nature never intended different species to grow from the same root.

The appeal of the lush floral Hawaiian patterns has spread well beyond the islands. British quilter Edyth Henry discovered the style in the early 1980s and has taught many other quilters how to design and cut their own Hawailan patterns. She explains her love of the style by saying:

SPIRIT OF MY PLACE

Julie Haddrick

South Australia, Australia

2002

72 × 79"

(184 × 201 cm)

Overflowing with a wealth of flowers such as the Dutch iris, arum lilies, nasturtiums—all indigenous plants to Australia—this quilt is stitched in Julie's own hand-dyed and painted fabrics. It was juried into the Bernina World Quilt Competition and Exhibition, USA, 2002.

As I keep telling people, Hawaiian appliqué is the easiest kind of applique there is. No fiddly little pieces to be fitted under others. There is only one piece and once it is cut and tacked in place, it is just a case of keeping on going until you get to the end!

STAINED GLASS APPLIQUÉ

With this form of appliqué, the edges of applied motifs are covered with a bias binding. This covers the raw edges of the appliqué, and eliminates the need for needleturn stitching. It also accentuates each part of the pattern, imitating the artistry of stained glass windows, hence its name. Contemporary quiltmakers who use this technique take inspiration from a variety of sources, such as the sumptuous patterns apparent in Louis Comfort Tiffany's art glass from the late nineteenth and early twentieth centuries, as well as other Art Nouveau decorative arts. The more spare designs of Modernist architects, such as Charles Rennie Mackintosh or Frank Lloyd Wright, are also ideal for interpretation in stained glass appliqué. Mackintosh's favorite floral motif was the rose, which he used in many of his stylized designs using a variety of media—leaded glass, wood, watercolor, stenciled fabric, base and precious metals. The everyday decorative leaded lights often seen in glazed doors and windows provided ready designs for the quilter as shown in Julie Haddrick's quilt, *Spirit of my Place* (page 43). This quilt has a wealth of symbolism personal to the quiltmaker.

GLASGOW STYLE
Mavis Haslam
Kent, England
1988
58 × 32"
(147 × 81 cm)

During visits to Glasgow,
Mavis was impressed by
the wealth of stained
glass in the sandstone
houses and the dramatic
designs of Charles
Rennie Mackintosh, the
city's famous architect
and designer. This
inspired her original
design, the first in a
series of quilts. The bias
binding is hand
appliquéd and is used to
clearly define the
individual petals in each
flower. This quilt was
awarded second prize at
the National Patchwork
Championships, UK,
1988.

CLEMATIS

Barbara Disbrowe

Hertfordshire, England

2002

23 × 21" (59 × 53 cm)

In the clematis plant, the color comes from the sepals as there are no true petals. Several leaves are free-hanging, made by sandwiching stabilizer between two layers of fabric. Machine stitching defines the veins in the leaves.

For example, the top section recalls the theme of Australian settlement through its depiction of a federation window seen from her grandparents' home.

With this technique, the bias binding is usually black for maximum contrast. Because the technique produces perfect curves and points, it is ideal for petals, leaves, and flowing stems. For quilters who want to achieve a natural effect, hand-dyed and painted fabrics are ideal for providing a gentle gradation of color. The main consideration when sewing this form of appliqué is to work out the sewing order for building up the individual elements. The raw end of each bias strip should be covered by subsequent lengths to give a neat finish.

TECHNIQUE
FOLK-ART HAND APPLIQUÉ
INSPIRED BY THE QUILT: FOLK-ART DAISY

FOLK-ART DAISY

Maker/s unknown, probably American, c. 1865

65 × 90½" (165 × 230 cm)

Unsubstantiated reports suggest that this quilt was sewn by freed Texan slaves shortly after the American Civil War ended in 1861. It is possible that the quilt had a number of makers because of the different appliqué motifs and the varying sizes of the patches. The majority of the 101 blocks feature perky pink and purple daisies cut from hat felt and blanket stitched onto the woolen fabric. However, there are a few odd blocks with tree-like motifs, butterflies and abstract forms in the shape of an M, the initial of the maker, maybe? Powerhouse Museum, Australia

This project is suitable for a beginner because minor differences in the positioning of motifs and stitch sizes are part of folk-art appliqué. Fleece is used for the flower petals and is an ideal fabric as it is easy to sew, does not fray and washes easily. This pattern has been taken directly from a block in the sixth row, but feel free to have fewer petals or cut different sizes. A top-stitching thread is used because it is thicker than normal thread and suits this appliqué

MATERIALS FOR ONE BLOCK

- 12 × 12" (30 × 30 cm) linen or cotton fabric
- 12 × 12" (30 × 30 cm) dark pink fleece
- Scrap of contrasting fleece
- Craft paper

- Cream top-stitching (button) thread
- Pins
- Needle
- Paper and fabric scissors

1 Fold the paper over 1½" (4 cm) from one edge. Cut six petal templates (page 144) from the paper and trim a fraction off one end to give a flatter edge. Pin onto the fleece and cut out six petals. There is no need to add any extra seam allowance. Press the background linen square.

2 Position petals in the center with the flatter edges toward the center. Pin in place. Blanket stitch around each petal. Do not pull the thread too tight as it would disappear into the pile of the fleece.

3 Cut a circle from the contrasting fleece large enough to cover the space at the center of all the petals. Pin in place and blanket stitch as above.

4 To complete the block, stitch the stem using a back stitch or stem stitch, starting at the center.

TECHNIQUE
FUSED APPLIQUÉ
INSPIRED BY THE QUILT: TULIP AND ROSES WREATH

TULIP AND ROSES WREATH

Unknown quiltmaker, probably USA c. 1860–1880

73 × 70" (185 × 178 cm)

A simple block, when repeated 25 times across a quilt, creates secondary patterns and confuses the eye as to the main focus of the design. Concentrate on the orange tulips and they advance as a pattern of four. Shift your gaze to the dark plant stems and red flowers and they become more prominent. There is a border of equal complexity, which includes the same design elements although some leaves have changed color—deliberately or due to running out of blue fabric perhaps? The stylized vine flows around three sides, but not the fourth. Presumably this indicates the top which was tucked behind the bedclothes.

University of Nebraska Collection

For quiltmakers today the use of a fusible adhesive (bonding agent) makes appliqué-ing complex shapes far simpler. The web is ironed onto the back of the fabric and the motif is cut out. This in turn is ironed onto the background fabric to produce a bonded appliqué without stitching. However, for permanence most quilters either machine satin stitch individually around each motif before assembling the different blocks or free stitch across the entire block at the quilting stage. For added interest hand-dyed fabric is used for the flower blooms for a subtle difference in each block.

MATERIALS FOR ONE BLOCK

- 18 × 18" (45 × 45 cm) background cotton fabric
- 10 × 10" (25 × 25 cm) orange cotton fabric
- 6 × 6" (15 × 15 cm) red cotton fabric
- 6 × 10" (15 × 25 cm) dark blue fabric
- Paper-backed fusible adhesive (bonding agent)
- Pencil
- Small fabric scissors

1 For each color of fabric, trace the pattern pieces from page 144 through to the paper side of the fusible adhesive (bonding agent) using a pencil. Move the web around to make the best use of space. You do not need to leave large gaps between the shapes.

2 Fuse the paper-backed adhesive (bonding agent) onto the wrong side of the fabric. Cut each shape on the pencil line. You do not need to allow extra for a seam allowance with this style of appliqué.

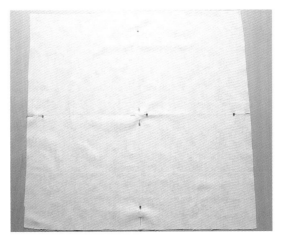

3 Cut out the background square and gently press in quarters to find the mid-points and the center. Unfold and mark with pins.

4 Peel the backing paper from the motifs. Position them, adhesive side down, on the background square, using the pins to help center the design.

5 Carefully remove all the pattern pieces except the tulips and buds. Remove the marking pins and fuse the motifs in place following the bonding manufacturer's instructions.

6 Place the blue wreath on top of the pressed tulips and red flowers on top of the blue wreath.

7 Fuse in position as above. Finally, press the leaves in place.

TECHNIQUE
FREEZER PAPER HAND APPLIQUÉ
INSPIRED BY THE QUILT: PRAIRIE ROSE

PRAIRIE ROSE

Eliza J Herron, probably Pennsylvania, USA, 1857

92 × 92" (234 × 234 cm)

This striking quilt features a bold plant with branches leading to small cactus-type flowers. The layout of this nine-block quilt is unusual, with eight of the plant blocks pointing toward the central stylized flower. The encircling vine in the outer border and bright red binding frame the quilt, and the simple leaf-and-berry motifs complement the vivid blocks. The dense quilted feathers echo the curve of the plant stems, with the rest of the background filled in with parallel lines of stitching. The two solid green fabrics in the quilt used have faded at different rates. The quiltmaker, Eliza J Herron, embroidered her name and the date 1857 on the lower central block.

University of Nebraska-Lincoln collection

In the original quilt each block measures about 24 inches. Here we have designed a simplified and smaller version of the block so you can practice appliqué using freezer paper. Contemporary quiltmakers have discovered that freezer paper or contact paper (designed for food storage) is ideal as an aid to prepare motifs for appliqué. With this method of appliqué, more time is spent in the preparation of the appliqué shapes in order to make the sewing easier and quicker. The main advantage is that the motifs keep both their shape and their folded edge so complicated shapes can be stitched more quickly.

MATERIALS FOR ONE BLOCK

- 15 × 18" (38 × 46 cm) neutral cotton fabric
- 5 × 10" (12 × 25 cm) red cotton fabric
- 8 × 10" (20 × 25 cm) dark green cotton fabric
- 6 × 10" (15 × 25 cm) leaf green cotton fabric
- Scrap of yellow fabric
- Template plastic
- Freezer paper
- Paper and fabric scissors
- Spray starch
- Small paint brush
- Pins or basting (tacking) thread
- Needle
- Matching thread

1 Trace the patterns from page 145 onto the template plastic and cut out the shapes. Note that all the leaves are the same size so you only need to draw and cut one from the plastic. Place on the paper side of the freezer paper, draw around in pencil, and cut out the required number of paper shapes for the block.

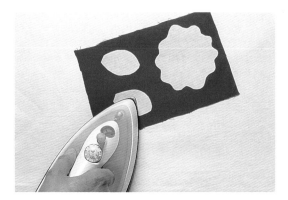

2 Position the freezer paper sticky side down on the wrong side of the fabric and iron in place, using a cotton heat setting. Cut around each shape allowing a ¼" (6 mm) allowance.

3 On concave edges or inner corners, snip into the seam allowance. Spray some of the spray starch liquid into its lid. Use the brush to paint starch onto the seam allowances, but not on the freezer paper.

4 Press the seam allowance around to the back of the freezer paper, pressing the tips of any leaves first. Use the side of the iron to fold in the rest of the material, pleating the fabric to achieve a smooth curve. Be careful not to burn your fingers.

5 Once the appliqué has cooled, peel off the freezer paper. The paper can be used several times if you are using multiple blocks.

6 If your background is a light colored fabric you can place the pattern underneath to help position the motifs. Pin or baste (tack) the motifs in place, starting with the plant and leaves. Appliqué in place by hand using small blind stitches (slipstitch) and a toning thread color.

7 If you use the sewing machine, choose a slipstitch (blind stitch) and an invisible (monofilament) thread.

PIECED QUILTS

Converting nature's curves and angles into a straight-line geometric puzzle that can be pieced together is a challenge that quiltmakers have successfully tackled for more than 200 years. When viewed at a distance, pieced quilts often give the optical illusion of rounded lines. Recent technical developments in patchwork, such as foundation piecing, allow quilters to sew minute shapes into a complex overall pattern.

FLOWER BASKET PETIT POINT

Grace McCance Snyder

Nebraska, USA

1942–1943

94 × 92"

(239 × 234 cm)

The pieced square and triangular patches are arranged in 13 blocks, with eight border triangles containing roses. Note the variation in these blocks which have been designed to link up with the outer rose vine and checkerboard border. Grace started to piece quilt blocks as a child in the 1880s. She hand pieced and quilted her petit point masterpiece in only 16 months. In 1999 the quilt was selected as one of the Twentieth Century's Best American Quilts.

Nebraska State Historical Society

**GRANDMOTHER'S
FLOWER BASKET**

The Weyward Quilters
Surrey, England
2002
102 × 108"
(259 × 274 cm)

This incredible quilt was
sewn by four friends, all
new to quiltmaking, to
raise funds for a
hospice. Inspired by a
quilt shown in a 1979
book *Quilts of America*
by Erica Wilson, the
colors were changed to
produce this delightful
pastel quilt reminiscent
of the 1930s. The
hexagon patches form
the rosettes within the
central basket, while the
hexagons in the border
are arranged in a
diamond pattern.
Collection of Vera Moles

PIECED FLORAL QUILTS CAN BE PLACED into five main categories depending on their appearance or construction. These are single patch or mosaic quilts, repeating block patterns, tessellated designs, foundation piecing, and scenic quilts. Like any type of creative work, each type of piecing goes through fashions, with a rise and fall in popularity. In addition, the techniques or styles can be combined, such as *Silk Nosegays* by Estelle Morin (page 61) which features a repeating block motif constructed with foundation piecing.

The block format was especially favored by nineteenth-century American quiltmakers and was usually sewn in a square, which was repeated across the quilt. Within this category there are a number of flower, leaf, and tree blocks that vary in degrees of complexity. For example, the simple Periwinkle block uses a four-patch layout, whereas the Japanese Poppy pattern is based on a 100-patch-block.

In recent years, quiltmakers who are working in a more contemporary style have reinterpreted the pieced floral quilt using new techniques, such as foundation (paper) piecing, tessellations of a single patch, and a more pictorial style with one single image rather than the traditional repeating-block motif.

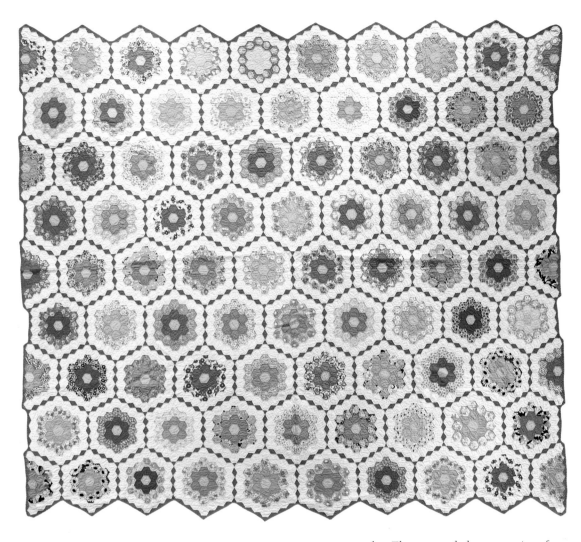

GRANDMOTHER'S FLOWER GARDEN VARIATION
Maker and origin unknown
1930s
74 × 84"
(188 × 213 cm)

A single glance at the color scheme proclaims this quilt to be a 1930s creation. The fabrics have been carefully chosen in these double hexagon rosettes. All the patterned fabrics form complete outer rings, except for a bold daisy-like black-eyed Susan. The fabrics have been "fussy cut" to show the flower on each hexagon. Collection of Patricia Cox Crews

GRANDMOTHER'S FLOWER GARDEN

From a piecing point of view, the easiest format (although not necessarily the quickest) is the one-patch block in which a single geometric patch is used across the quilt surface. The most common design in this category is called Grandmother's Flower Garden and is made up of hexagonal patches. Many quilters who started quilting in the 1970s and 1980s, at the beginning of the current revival, cut their "quilting teeth" on a hexagon quilt.

This mosaic pieced design has been popular for 200 years, and the sewn blocks resemble a bold flower with six petals. The design is created by repeating hexagonal patches. The hexagons usually are the same length on all six sides. It is also possible to piece elongated hexagons, which have two longer sides which creates a different visual pattern. The patches are sewn as a block of seven; six patches surround a center patch. The central hexagon is often in a plain fabric for maximum contrast if the surrounding hexagons are patterned, or vice versa (see the *Grandmother's Flower Garden Variation* on this page). This initial block can be surrounded by a second or third row of hexagons. The large blocks are then sewn together using a row of hexagons, all in the same color, often white. This clearly defines each separate flower garden block. Alternatively, diamonds can be used to separate the blocks, creating a variation of the main pattern called Garden Path. The *Flower Garden Mosaic* quilt on page 73 shows how the hexagons can be arranged in concentric rings of different colors. For maximum effect on fabrics with larger patterns, quilters will often position templates centrally over a motif such as a flower head so that it appears in the middle of the sewn patch. This practice is

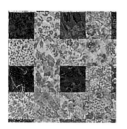

**SEASONAL
GARDENS**

Deirdre Amsden
London, England
1998
Each quilt 26½ × 26½"
(67 × 67 cm)

The subtle merging of
patterns makes these
four quilts seem to
shimmer as if in a
summer heatwave. The
central, darker squares
(each 1 ¾" or 4½ cm)
represent the structure
of formal gardens, with
flowerbeds and paving
stones. These defined
shapes break down
toward the outer edges
just as the natural
countryside has few
lines and no rigidity of
design.

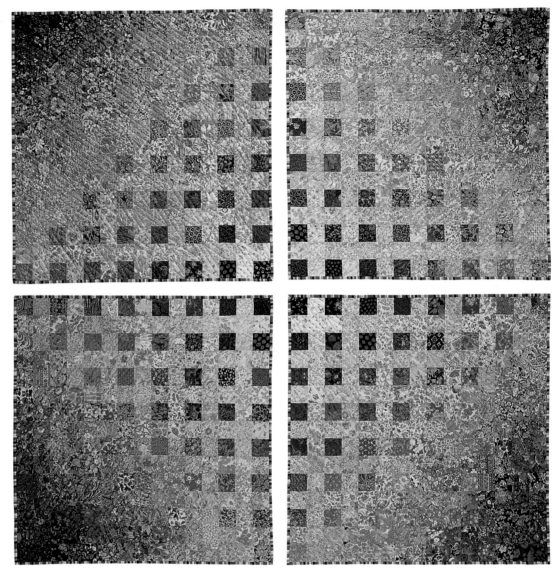

known as fussy cutting and uses more fabric because the hexagon templates are not butted up against one another when the patches are cut.

Because of the geometry of the patch shape, hand piecing is easier than machine sewing. In Britain, patches are traditionally folded and basted (tacked) over a paper or card template which is cut to the finished size of the patch. Patches are sewn together by hand with small oversewing stitches. The templates are kept in the quilt until the top is fully sewn. It is then a lengthy task to pull out the basting (tacking) stitches and remove all the hexagon templates. This style of patchwork became known as English Piecing, although faster methods of stitching are preferred by quiltmakers today. In America the hexagon quilt design is also popular, although the piecing together of patches is done with a running stitch and no basted (tacked) template. Because of this, the hexagon patches is generally larger for easier sewing.

According to Amelia Peck, author of *American Quilts and Coverlets*, this classic geometric pattern had a resurgence of popularity in the 1870s and 1880s because of Moorish and Turkish influences. Fifty years later in the 1920s and 1930s, many American newspapers and magazines published quilt patterns and the Grandmother's Flower Garden was a frequently published block.

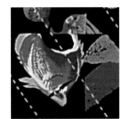

FOCAL POINT III
Deirdre Amsden
London, England
1998
Each quilt 34 × 24"
(86 × 61 cm)

These quilts are based
on the poem *Experience*,
by Christopher Leach,
which describes the
impact of viewing things
quickly from a train
window and then in
closer detail. The sharp
visual division between
the four areas and the
graduating color within
each section stems
entirely from Deirdre's
preoccupation with tone.

POPPY

Patricia Archibald
West Lothian, Scotland
1992
35 × 35" (89 × 89 cm)

A pencil sketch evolved
into this original stylized
design with half-square
triangles forming 3" (7½
cm) blocks. One quarter
of the sketch was
modified and turned 90°
to create the pattern.

Quilts from these decades are recognizable because of their distinctive candy-colored schemes, often incorporating white and bright mint green.

MOSAIC QUILTS

Rather like a child's box of wooden mosaic shapes, the building blocks of a quilt can be very simple, such as squares and right-angled triangles. Such designs occurred frequently in English scrap quilts of the past, and the format has been rediscovered by contemporary quilters. When the patchwork shape is common throughout the quilt, the quilter is free to use the color and pattern in a fabric to create the illusion of a floral design. However, it takes great skill to view fabrics as a color palette in the same way an artist views a paintbox. The relative lightness and darkness (shade) and grayness versus brightness (tone) of a fabric are crucial to the final design.

Many quilters working with mosaic quilts use one of three design methods to plan their quilt. First, a design can be drawn to scale on paper, which is then shaded with color pencils in order to aid the placing of fabrics. Computer programs, such as EQ5 and Quilt Pro, have speeded up this planning and design process. Quilters can change colors at the click of a mouse and produce a number of design options in a fraction of the time. This software uses fabric patterns from a swatch library as scanned fabrics from the quilter's collection, to produce a realistic model of the finished quilt. Such design

CAROLINA LILY

(right)

Audrey Miller

Berkshire, England

2003

96 × 67"

(244 × 170 cm)

DAHLIA

(below)

Nicole Demol

Villiers en Plaine, France

2002

47 × 47"

(120 × 120 cm)

The cream print has been "fussy cut" so the kingfishers and convolvulus flowers appear at the center of each of the patches.

planning saves time at the sewing stage and avoids visual surprises related to areas of the quilt which are not successful in terms of fabric shade and tone.

A more improvisational method of design involves cutting a variety of patches and arranging them on a table or flannel-covered design wall. The design wall allows the quilt to be viewed vertically rather than horizontally, which distorts perspective. Cotton fabric patches adhere to the flannel surfaces without pins. Once the pattern is laid out there is usually a long period of rearranging as tones and values are swapped to accentuate or merge areas of color.

The well-known British quilt artist, Deirdre Amsden, has been developing this method since the 1970s. Her pioneering quilt style has given rise to the term "watercolor" or "color-wash" quilts, because the subtle printed fabrics take on a painted appearance as patterns blend in an overall colorwash. Deirdre is well-known for her use of highly patterned, floral lawn fabrics, particularly those from

Liberty of London. Her quilts represent a microcosm of floral designs over several decades. As Deirdre explains in *Quilter's Newsletter Magazine*, September 2001:

The prints lose some of their identity when cut into small pieces, allowing me to use them like paint. The irregular splashes of color provided by the variety of prints help disguise the seams, making the image seem continuous, not pieced.

Visually, mosaic patchwork can create an abstract study of nature. The impression may be of flowers viewed at a distance, much like Monet's watercolor paintings, or the quilt can have the rather chaotic look of a multicolored herbaceous border at the height of summer, when flowers jostle for space in the flowerbed and colors cheerfully clash with each other.

Inspiration for such floral quilts can come directly from nature and from observing gardens changing through the seasons. Upon retirement, or "gardening leave" as it is also known, British quilter Jinny Jarry found she could spend more time in her

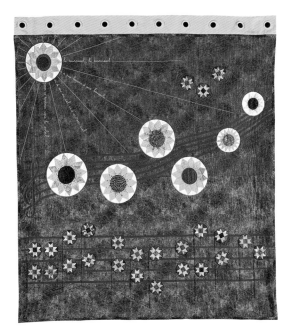

garden and enjoy the changing colors of flowers throughout the year. Her quilt, *Gardening Leave*, (page 76) was based on her close observation of delphiniums growing against a garden wall. Continuing her floral theme, Jinny has sewn a second quilt, based on the dramatic floral fashions of British designer Alexander McQueen. It is interesting to note that McQueen's fashion collection for 2004 includes garments made from pieced Grandmother's Flower Garden blocks, reminding us that life imitates art.

During the nineteenth and early twentieth century, china that was transfer printed with busy all-over designs was immensely popular. Called chintzware, it provided plenty of

SUNFLOWERS
(left)
Nicole Demol
Villiers en Plaine, France
2002
80 × 67"
(202 × 170 cm)

This quilt uses a variety of piecing techniques. The mini-blocks represent musical notes for a song by Nana Mouskouri about sunflowers reaching for the light.

SILK NOSEGAYS
Estelle Morin
Levallois-Perret, France
1999
29½ × 29½"
(75 × 75 cm)

Nosegay is a traditional block (also called French Bouquet or Bride's Bouquet) found on many 1930s quilts. It was often sewn in the decade's favored colors of yellow, mint, and light purple. The colors used here and the radiating arrangement give the impression of a Christmas wreath.

BOTANICAL GARDEN

Anja Townrow

Walsall, England

2003

48 × 48"

(120 × 120 cm)

Anja is well-known for her foundation-pieced flower designs. The use of Bali batik fabrics, which have mottled and variegated patterns, gives the blooms added vitality. In this wall quilt, horticultural convention is put to one side as spiky pink gladioli (bottom right) bloom side by side with a marigold (center) and a venus flytrap (top right). The quilt was machine quilted with metallic rayon thread.

floral inspiration but was difficult to use in quilt designs because of its busyness. However, china patterns derived from needlepoint were far easier to adapt for piecing because quilters could base their designs quite literally on the china pattern, since the colors had already been subdivided into smaller, regular units. *Flower Basket Petit Point* by Grace McCance Snyder (page 54) is an excellent example of a pieced floral design. Grace's original design was based on a china pattern by German artist Wendelin Grossman for the Salem China Company in America. The quilt contains 85,789 square or triangular patches. When sewn together, eight triangles form a block the size of a postage stamp! Not

surprisingly the quilt was chosen by a committee of 24 quilting experts as one of the Twentieth Century's Best American Quilts at the turn of the millennium.

REPEATING BLOCKS

Until the 1890s, quilt block names were not standardized and it is not uncommon to find the same block design called very different names. One example is the Carolina Lily, also known as the Virginia Lily, North Carolina Lily, Meadow Lily, and the Double Tulip. The three flowerhead sections are composed of four diamonds and a triangle. Variations occur with the style of the appliquéd stem and the shape of the lower

leaves. Many nineteenth-century examples of the lily block used red and green fabric against a plain cream or white background. The quilt blocks are usually set on point and facing in one direction so that the flowers point skywards. However, the blocks may point toward the center, lengthwise, or in a mirror-type arrangement. The Carolina Lily is also similar to the less common Poinsettia pieced pattern which tends to have three flower stems per block. Unlike many floral designs where it seems "more is better," the graceful lily design works well with large spaces between the blocks.

Two of the most useful geometric shapes for patchwork flowers are the diamond and the triangle. These simple shapes can become fully opened flowers, buds, or leaves. Larger patches can easily be sewn together using American-style piecing in which patches are placed in pairs, right sides together, and sewn using a ¼-inch (6 mm) seam allowance. In any block, it is helpful to break down design into smaller sewing units such as two diamonds or two triangles. These units are then combined to build the finished block. When sewing diamonds, a few patches will need to be inset; however, the majority of seams will be straight and will combine into larger triangle and square blocks. Nicole Demol's quilt, *Sunflowers*, (page 61) is a modern, pieced interpretation of a flower whose bright and

A TASTE OF SUMMER
Annette Morgan
Suffolk, England
2001
79 × 79"
(201 × 201 cm)

A traditional patchwork pattern, such as the graphic Coming Up Sunshine block, can be successfully reinterpreted in a contemporary floral quilt. The four foundation-pieced blocks in each corner complement both the medallion-style format and the vine of appliquéd flowers that resemble simple paper-cuts. This quilt won first place for large wall hanging, Quilts UK, 2001, and an Honorable Mention at the World Quilt and Textile Fair, USA, 2001.

**TROPICAL
TESSELLATION**
Round Robin Quilters
Berkshire, England
2000
59 × 85"
(150 × 216 cm)

The nine Round Robin
group members
designed their quilt after
seeing a similar
technnique used by
quilter Jinny Beyer. The
design is based on a 60°
diamond subdivided into
six strips. The depth of
color in each block and
the proportion of red
to green, gives the
impression of hothouse
flowers in bud, half
open, or in full bloom.
Free machine quilted
petals and leaves
enhance the design, and
flower centers are
defined with
embroidery thread.
Royal Berks Hospital
collection

gaudy heads have fascinated quilters over the centuries. In Nicole's quilt, textured fabric gives the illusion of multiseeded heads and a multitude of yellow petals sewn from diamonds and triangles.

For beginners, curved piecing is more difficult to sew than patches with straight lines. Proficient quilters can piece designs with curved patches (such as *Texas Star Tulip* page 66) which less experienced stitchers may have to do in appliqué. Another advantage of curved piecing is that the petal-shaped templates give a very realistic effect for floral quilts, as shown in another quilt by Nicole Demol, the *Dahlia* quilt (page 60). This pattern is an old favorite and Nicole was inspired to sew her vibrant design by the book *The Quick and Easy Giant Dahlia* by Murvin and Payne. The intricate piecing comprises a 16-point star at the center, surrounded by 16 curved, pieced segments. When sewn in vibrant

colors, the effect is of a striking dahlia in full bloom.

Today, Amish quiltmakers sew Dahlia quilts (also known as Starflowers) in great numbers, particularly to non-Amish or "English" buyers. Completely different in appearance, the Amish Dahlia is based on a variation of the LeMoyne Star block in which eight individual petals are gathered at their bases and inserted under a circle of fabric. This gives the quilt a three-dimensional appearance.

While there are hundreds of pieced blocks with stylized flower designs, many types of blocks can be worked into a floral quilt, depending on their setting and the fabrics chosen. *North Shore Beauties* by Canadian quilter Jennifer Cooper (page 8) is an ideal example of a pieced block called New York Beauty, popular in the Art Deco era, which is reinventing itself as a flower block. By sewing four blocks together, Jennifer created giant spiky flowers reminiscent of dahlias and spider chrysanthemums. Bold floral print fabrics add weight to the visual illusion. Similar effects can be created with other classic blocks, such as Dresden Plate, Orange Peel, and all manner of star blocks.

FOUNDATION PIECING

For quilters wanting to work with more complex designs or on a small scale, foundation piecing is an interesting option. The popularity of foundation piecing is largely due to the teaching and books of Carol Doak, Margaret Rolfe and Anja Townrow, published since the mid 1990s. This style of piecing, where the design is drawn (traced) on backing

FLORAL TESSELLATION
Barbara Middlebrook
Isle of Wight, England
2001
61 × 51½"
(155 × 131 cm)

Barbara's hand-dyed fabrics create a rich range of bright summer colors. Use of a thicker thread in the machine-quilted petal shapes gives the illusion of flower heads, although many of the patches are actually squared off.

SWEET SWEET RAIN
Toyoko Miyajima
Nagano, Japan
2000
72 × 72"
(184 × 184 cm)

This incredible patchwork quilt is sewn and quilted by hand and contains 6,400 pieces. The quilt perfectly captures the subtle color changes that occur as the hydrangea blooms emerge.

TEXAS STAR TULIP

Maker unknown
Probably USA
c. 1860–80
87 × 71"
(221 × 180 cm)

The frequent use of tulips in quilts reflects the popularity of this bulb during the nineteenth century. Most tulip quilts are appliquéd. However, this entire design is pieced, using curved shapes.
University of Nebraska-Lincoln

POT GROWN

Anja Townrow
Walsall, England
2002
84 × 64"
(210 × 160 cm)

foundation of either paper or stabilizer, allows precise sewing of tiny patches through the sew-and-flip method. Razor-sharp points are achievable, which are essential for patterns such as Mariner's Compass, a nautical block which quilters such as Margaret Docherty and Annette Morgan have effectively converted into floral patterns. Foundation-piecing can strengthen fragile or delicate fabrics that might otherwise be difficult to sew. In *Silk Nosegays* by Estelle Morin of France (page 61), a series of triangles are foundation-pieced onto stabilizer using a technique taught by Carol Doak. The interfacing stabilizes the dupion silk fabric which otherwise has a tendency to fray.

COMPLEX PIECING

For experienced quilters wanting a challenge, complicated pieced blocks can be designed to create lifelike fabric flowers. American quilt artist Ruth McDowell can take the credit for advancing many quilters' technical skills in drafting such patterns. Ruth's detailed blocks tackle many of the most popular flowers—roses, irises, and lilies—as well as the more unusual hollyhocks, waterlilies, and sweet peas.

Starting with a photograph, a tracing is made and enlarged to the desired size of the block. This is broken down into sections using straight lines. The resulting block contains many irregular shapes and a logical mind is needed to work out the piecing order. By using curved and inset piecing of varying difficulty, each pattern piece can be joined with its neighbor, finally creating a realistic flower block. An illusion of a curved leaf or petal is created by minute changes of angles on the seams. The quilter has to think about where seams intersect (to avoid bulkiness) and have a talent for seeing the potential in plaids, texture patterns, and print fabrics rather than obvious floral designs. As McDowell explains in her book *Expanding the Basics* (1998):

There have been many fabrics manufactured recently to solve some of the difficulties in translating nature into fabric quilts. Probably because of my contrary nature, I can't stand to use most of these. Or at least to use them as their designers intended.

HYDRANGEA FENCE

Dilys Fronks
Flintshire, Wales
2000
46 × 42"
(117 × 107 cm)

One of Dilys' extensive "wrought iron" series, this quilt gives the illusion of looking from the shade of a tree, past a decorative wrought iron fence to a bank of pink, blue and purple hydrangea bushes. The sky and distant hydrangeas are strip-pieced and machine quilted. Flowers in the foreground are machine appliquéd. The fence is applied last, using a needleturn technique and a concealed stitch.

TESSELLATED PATCHWORK

The simplest definition of a tessellated patchwork design is one in which a single geometric motif is repeated indefinitely across a surface without any gaps. Each piece fits into its neighboring patch, rather like a jigsaw puzzle that has only one type of interlocking unit. The blocks can be constructed in a number of ways. One method in which squares are cut and resewn in a random order is described by Martha Thompson in her book *Squaredance*. A square template is marked and cut, then placed on the pieced quilt top at an angle of 57°. This cuts across the previously sewn lines.

The angled squares are cut and resewn in the same order (this is very important) to form a new pattern in which the blocks twist rather like a child's windmill.

When this technique is repeated on a large enough scale, the overall effect can be like an Impressionist painting. Japanese quiltmaker Toyoko Miyajima has created possibly the ultimate example of this technique with her masterpiece *Sweet Sweet Rain* (page 65) which captures the sensation of hydrangea *Ajisai* blooms at the height of summer. Toyoko explains that the floral quilt inspiration dates back to her childhood:

**BLUEBELLS AT
DUSK**

Barbara Weeks

Hertfordshire, England

1997

32 × 24" (82 × 62 cm)

Barbara used her own
dyed and painted silk
and cotton for this floral
landscape, one in a
series of five inspired by
the paintings of Klimt
and a local bluebell
forest. The quilts explore
the element of surprise
created when familiar
surroundings are viewed
in changing light at
different times of the
day. The silver birch bark
contrasts with the lush
color on the woodland
floor. Dense free-
machine quilting adds to
the feeling of closely
packed flowers and
leaves.

*I liked rain very much as a child because my father
and mother would then return from the farm.
Looking at the rain, I waited for them in anticipation.
The Ajisai in the yard became wet with raindrops
and even now, if I look at an Ajisai I remember my
childhood with nostalgia.*

A typical tessellated pattern is the traditional
Tumbling Blocks design made from interlocking
60° diamonds. With their vibrant quilt
Tropical Tessellation (page 64) the Round
Robin quilt group created a more complex
variation of the Tumbling Block design.
They machine pieced six strips to form
the diamond, using the flip-and-turn method.

This allowed them to manipulate the colors within each block to create spiky, abstract flower heads.

LANDSCAPE QUILTS

The landscape or scenic quilt is best suited to more experienced quilters who are capable of drafting their own original pieced designs. This particular style of work is a recent development because more quiltmakers now sew quilts for walls than for beds. They therefore approach a project in much the same way a painter would. They view it as a flexible canvas for their own self-expression. With this particular style of floral quilt the overall impression is more important than the individual plant, flower head, or composite parts. For a realistic impression, perspective is very important. Quilts created from personal experiences and private observation generally have far more character and individuality, so close observation of nature is essential as is a photographic record of the changes in growing plants over the seasons. Photographs can also be of great help when choosing or dyeing fabrics, as they record in detail the subtle changes in tone and shade that memory alone cannot always provide.

Dilys Fronks' *Hydrangea Fence* (page 67) has the appeal of an Impressionist painting and

SPRING BOUQUET
Yoko Komine
Tokyo, Japan
2000
79 × 79"
(200 × 200 cm)

This cheerful quilt has a central tulip bouquet, inspired by a book by Eijun Takahashi. This is bordered by 36 pieced and appliquéd posy baskets. The trellis effect of the outer blocks frames the central design, and the bright prints and daisy border add to its folk-art appeal.

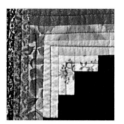

FLOWERS IN THE CABIN

Pam Clarke

Washington, USA

1998

105 × 105"

(267 × 267 cm)

This 16-block quilt has a real "scrappy" feel because of the variety of fabrics used. The machine-pieced logs are in different widths, 1 and 1½" (2½ and 3½ cm), so a slight illusion of a gentle curve is created. This also gives more room for the flower patterns which have been carefully positioned to exploit the available space. The flowers are sewn using reverse appliqué, and edges are covered with blanket stitch. A pennant-style border is created by the half-square triangles.

recalls the colorwashes of Monet's paintings. Her quilts feature both piecing and appliqué. To achieve the watercolor effect in the background she uses both sides of the fabric. For Dilys, the appeal of floral motifs in quilts is largely due to their never-ending rainbow of colors, the endless possibilities of presentation, and the flexibility of the soft and forgiving shapes. As she explains, they do not all have to be perfect! The inspiration for this particular quilt came from her glimpse of some beautiful hydrangea flowers growing in her village in North Wales. The Welsh for hydrangea is *tri lliw ar ddeg*, which translates literally as "three colors on ten," This is certainly a perfect description of the layer upon layer of deepening and receding shades of color on this multihued shrub.

In contrast, Barbara Weeks' quilt *Bluebells at Dusk* (page 68) is more abstract. The bluebell flowers are not depicted in a lifelike way but by squares of fabric attached using raw-edge-bonded machine appliqué. Nevertheless, her lilac carpet of bulbs is instantly recognizable by anyone fortunate enough to have experienced such a springtime sight. The importance of merging color within the fabrics is important for landscape quilts, as nature is not known for its sharp edges and harsh color changes but rather its soft gradations of shade and tone.

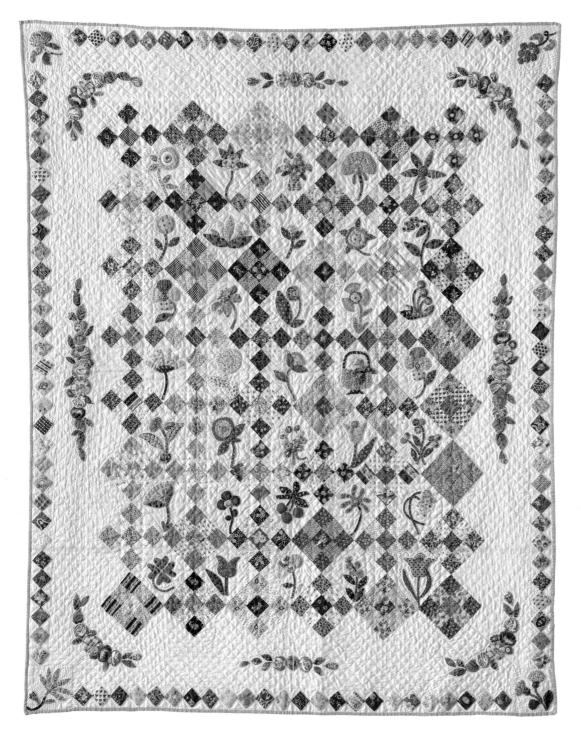

CALICO GARDEN

Florence Peto

New Jersey, USA

1952

49 × 39"

(124 × 99 cm)

This quilt is deceptive in size as each of the 48 nine-patch blocks is less than 3" (7½ cm square). These border 25 squares featuring a glorious selection of appliquéd flowers, including pansies, water lilies, marigolds, and a rogue bunch of cherries near the bottom. The wide range of cotton prints contributes to the liveliness of the quilt. This quilt was voted as one of America's 100 Best Quilts of the Twentieth Century. Shelburne Museum

PIECED AND APPLIQUÉD QUILTS

For many years piecing and appliqué have been used together for maximum effect in floral quilts. The flexibility of appliqué is complemented by the more formal nature of piecing. Two approaches for using this combination are to create a landscape quilt with a single image or to integrate traditional quilt formats and block designs with appliqué motifs.

The patchwork blocks can act as a frame for appliqué swags and wreaths, as shown by *Flowers in the Cabin* by Pam Clarke (page 70). In this quilt, the plain black Log Cabin strips provide a simple backdrop for the appliqué motifs. However, it should also be remembered that it is more difficult to appliqué onto a pieced background than onto a single piece of fabric. This is because of the extra seams. It is important to take care

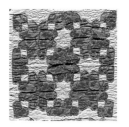

FLOWERPOTS FOR RUTH WATSON'S WEDDING

Maker unknown
Probably County
Durham, England
c. 1888
100 × 100"
(254 × 254 cm)

The vibrant appliqué center features eight wobbly vases in two shapes containing folk-art-style flower arrangements in khaki, red, and mint green fabric. A wide inner "border" is pieced using two patterns, Single Irish Chain and Diamond in the Square. Rather like the picture framer's trick of positioning a small painting in a large frame for emphasis, the patchwork succeeds in drawing attention to the central appliqué.
Bowes Museum

when positioning light colors in the corners of each Log Cabin block, as well as in the final logs in darker colors. This produces a bold frame for the flowers, which are one of the most important features in this colorful and vibrant quilt.

Alternatively, the patchwork and appliqué can have equal importance because of the colors and fabrics used and the relative size and positioning of the two types of blocks. This is clearly illustrated in the *Calico Garden* quilt by Florence Peto (page 71). The fabrics are more subdued and the cream background provides less of a contrast for the appliqué buds and flowers. In many of the nine-patch blocks small prints have an off-white or cream background. The blocks merge visually rather than having a sharp separation. This equality of design continues toward the outside of the quilt. The inner cream border has eight broderie perse swags, and the final edging is mostly pieced with four appliquéd corners.

TECHNIQUE
PAPER PIECING

INSPIRED BY THE QUILT: FLOWER GARDEN MOSAIC

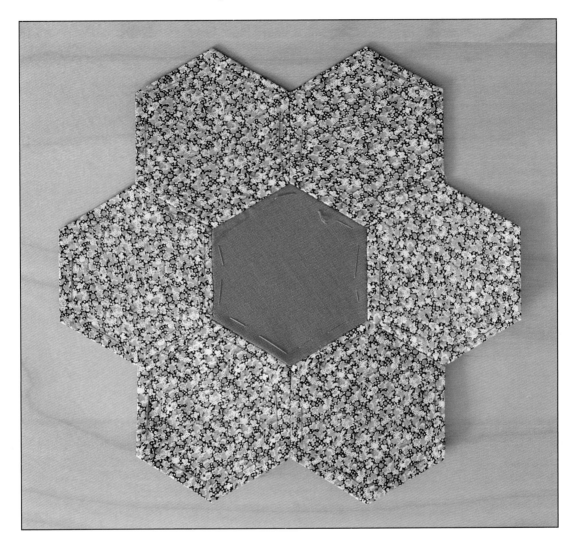

FLOWER GARDEN MOSAIC

Unknown quiltmaker, USA, c. 1870–90, 86 × 80" (218 × 203 cm)

The colors and fabrics in the center of this quilt from New England were carefully planned by the unknown nineteenth century quiltmaker to create a series of concentric hexagons separated by a patterned light orange fabric. Despite running out of matching fabric for the corner hexagons, fabrics of an equal tone have been used to create a harmonious pattern. The border is unusual and almost at odds with the precision in the central portion. The top left and bottom right corners show how the border blocks were not calculated to the correct length and needed trimming.

University of Nebraska-Lincoln

English paper piecing is suitable for portable patchwork projects, perhaps to be sewn alongside other faster projects. Once the paper templates and fabric patches are cut, they can be carried in a small bag with some threaded needles and hand sewn as time allows, for example, while travelling, waiting, or during other "dead" times. The small patch size allows you to include a variety of scraps to complete the rosettes.

MATERIALS FOR ONE BLOCK

- 3½ × 4" (9 × 10 cm) plain cotton fabric
- 7½ × 12" (19 × 30 cm) patterned cotton fabric
- Template plastic
- Paper or light cardstock for templates
- Pins
- Needle
- Toning thread and basting thread
- Paper and fabric scissors

1   Sort out and select fabrics, using a contrasting color for the center hexagon. For longevity, all the fabrics should be of an equal weight to ensure that seams do not pull because of stress.

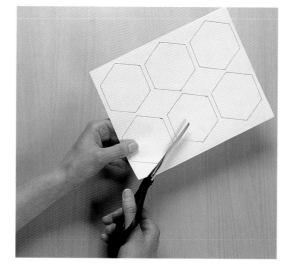

2   Trace the hexagon from page 146 onto the template plastic. Cut out carefully and use this as your master template. Cut enough paper templates—you will need one for each fabric patch. Iron all the fabric and cut out the patches allowing an extra ¼" (5 mm) seam allowance.

3   Place the paper template centrally on the reverse of the fabric patch and pin. Fold over the fabric evenly, ensuring the corners are neatly folded. Baste (tack) folded fabric in place. If knots are on the right side of the fabric, they are easier to remove later.

4 Place right sides of the center hexagon and one of the surrounding hexagons together and whip stitch along one edge with toning thread. Take care not to sew through the paper template.

5 Add another patterned hexagon next to the first and stitch to the central patch.

6 Add the remaining four patches. Then gently fold the center hexagon so that you can whipstitch each pair of outer patches. For stability the template papers should remain in the patches until adjoining rosettes are sewn together.

TECHNIQUE
CATHEDRAL WINDOW PATCHWORK
INSPIRED BY THE QUILT: GARDENING LEAVE

GARDENING LEAVE

Jinny Jarry, Bedfordshire, England, 2001

26½ × 21" (67 × 53 cm)

Jinny has used repeating Cathedral Window and Secret Garden design units to create an abstract wall quilt based on the colors of delphiniums. Usually this folded patchwork is arranged in a more formal medallion layout with rows of changing colors. However, Jinny let the technique play second fiddle to the use of color to create a glorious wash of pinks, blues and purples across the quilt. For added interest, she used a variety of fabrics—including hand-dyed cottons, velvet, acetate, and loosely woven silk rather like muslin. In selected patches she inserted an additional fabric. This makes the design more difficult to dissect for the nonquilter because the inserts cover the seams between the folded, hand-sewn blocks.

Cathedral Window and Secret Garden patchwork is rather like a complex origami pattern in which squares of fabric are folded, turned, and refolded. The patches are sewn together by hand and the edges rolled back to produce a multilayered, textured surface reminiscent of the elaborate costumes of Tudor England. The design can appear complex for the nonquilter to decipher as extra squares of contrasting fabric can be inserted in the folded windows. The patchwork does not need a separate backing, and the final stitching of the rolled back edges produces a quilted effect when the stitches go all the way through to the reverse layer.

MATERIALS FOR ONE BLOCK

- Main color fabric at least 13 × 13"
  (32 × 32 cm)
- Scraps of toning and contrasting fabrics, each of
  at least 2 × 2" (5 × 5 cm)
- Rotary cutter with board
- Pins
- Iron for pressing
- Needle
- Matching threads
- 5½" (14 cm) pressing template

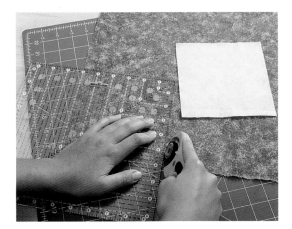

1 Cut 6" (15 cm) square of main fabric using the template as a guide.

2 Use template to fingerpress seam allowance. This should be done with both fabrics.

3 Fold diagonally to find the center of the main fabric. Fold opposite corners to meet at center. Press each fold in place. Your patch should now be about 4 × 4" (10 × 10 cm).

4 Fold new corners into the center again and press each fold. At the center, carefully but firmly sew points down. Use matching thread, as the stitches will show. The square will now be about 2¾ × 2¾" (7 × 7 cm).

5 Repeat to create 3 more squares. Join the squares wrong (unfolded) sides together, whipstitching (oversewing) with matching thread. This seam will not show as it will be covered with "windows." (The threads can be left in the center to stitch down rolled edges later.)

6 From toning and contrasting scraps, cut window squares 2 × 2" (5 × 5 cm). Turn a window square diagonally over the seamed edge of two main fabric squares. If necessary, trim window very slightly to let it lie flat. Position quite a few scraps before stitching. You may want to change your original plan. Put your final selection in position.

7 Roll the edges of the main fabric over the window squares. You may have to trim the window very slightly if it wrinkles as you roll the edges over. Pin each side. Slipstitch (blindstitch) rolled edge with matching thread, but don't go all the way through to the background. Make two small stitches across the main fabric at each corner to give a crisp finish.

TECHNIQUE
BLOCK PATCHWORK
INSPIRED BY THE QUILT: PRINTEMPS

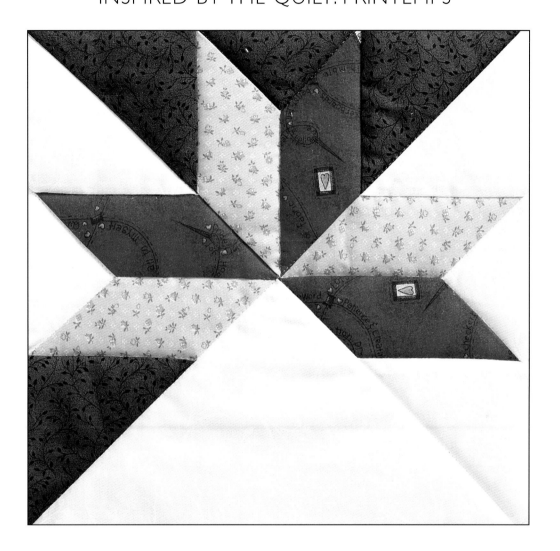

PRINTEMPS

Christine Moulin, Soisy-sur-Seine, France, 2000

108 × 95" (274 × 242 cm)

This original quilt design was created by Christine in response to a request by her daughter, Pauline, for a spring quilt with the colors of Monet's poppies. Each of the 20 flower groupings are in turn made up of eight triangles, subdivided and pieced in a windmill formation. Flashes of golden yellow and tomato red solid colors provide a foil for the busy floral prints. The large and small quilted petal shapes link all the blocks and the simple triple border.

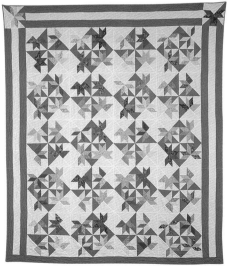

With traditional block patchwork, templates are traced onto the fabric. A ¼" (7.5 mm) seam allowance is added before cutting the patches, and the stitching is done on the pencil line. The seams are usually pressed in the direction of the darker fabric to prevent the shadow of a dark fabric from appearing under a lighter one. In all block patchwork the smallest elements are sewn together first to make larger units. This Printemps block offers a challenge because it has three inset triangles. Block patchwork can be sewn by hand or machine. If sewing by hand, start each seam with a knot and use a small running stitch.

1 Use templates on page 146. Mark and cut the fabric allowing ¼" (7.5 mm) seam allowance.

You will need: (letters appear on page 146)
• 3 Ws in yellow
• 3 Vs (or W reverse) in red
• 2 Ys in white
• 1 Y in green
• 2 Zs in green
• 1 Z in white
• 2 Xs (or Z reverse) in white
• 1 X (or Z reverse) in green
• 1 large triangle in white

MATERIALS FOR ONE BLOCK
• ⅛ yd (12 cm) red cotton fabric
• ⅛ yd (12 cm) yellow cotton fabric
• ⅛ yd (12 cm) green cotton fabric
• ⅛ yd (12 cm) white cotton fabric
• Fine pencil
• Pins
• Matching threads
• Sewing machine

2 Sew W to Z.
Sew V (W reverse) to X (Z reverse).
Press seams toward triangle. Using anchor stitch, sew W to Z (parallelogram and triangle) and sew W reverse to Z reverse. Join opposite pairs (normal and reverse).
Do NOT sew into seam allowances.
*Note: Anchor stitch = 2 stitches forward and 1 stitch back.

3 Sew inside of inset triangle Y into unit you have just made by sewing one side of the triangle to a W section. Then sew second side of the triangle Y. It is very important at this stage not to sew into the seam allowance.

4 Join the sections of the block together. Each time start stitching from the center point with an anchor stitch and then continue to the outside edge. Do not stitch across the center point. Check that all the seams meet precisely at the center and press these seams in a counter-clockwise direction.

5 Layer with batting (wadding) and backing fabric. Baste (tack) together avoiding the seams.

6 Machine quilt "in the ditch."

TECHNIQUE
FOUNDATION PIECING
INSPIRED BY THE QUILT: ROSE GARDEN

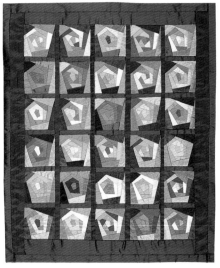

ROSE GARDEN

Estelle Morin, Levallois-Perret, France, 2002

22 × 18½" (56 × 47 cm)

This tiny patchwork captures an abstract view of an open rose surrounded by dark green leaves. The pattern is a Crazy Log Cabin which is foundation-pieced onto a non woven foundation material. Because of fabric color changes each 2½" (6½ cm) block appears to be very different. In fact, the pattern and piecing order is identical for all 30 blocks. Dupion and lightweight silks varying from pale blush pinks to dark burgundy red have been used. Sashing and a border in rich brown silk ties all the blocks together.

Log Cabin patchwork is usually made of strips around a central square, and crazy patchwork uses totally haphazard shapes fitted together in a random manner. By combining the two techniques a patchwork with a "controlled craziness" can be created. Foundation piecing is the ideal method for sewing irregular patches of fabric because the backing (whether fabric or a non-woven material such as stabilizer) helps to stabilize all the pieces regardless of whether or not they follow the grain of fabric. This project is suitable for hand or machine sewing by beginners or more experienced quilters.

MATERIALS FOR ONE BLOCK

- Light sew-in stabilizer
- Freezer paper
- Pencil
- Scraps of silk
- Flat flower pins
- Matching threads
- Sewing machine

1 Using the template shown on page 147, trace the pattern onto the stabilizer and the freezer paper using a light box. Mark the pieces in order to be sewn as shown on the template design. (Step shows stabilizer).

2 Cut the freezer paper along the traced lines and use as templates. Add ⅜" (1 cm) seam allowance around each template before cutting.

3 Place the first fabric piece right side up on the unmarked side of the stabilizer. Check to see that fabric covers the lines and pin in place.

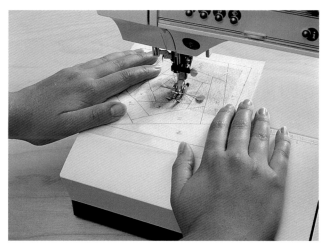

4 Place second fabric right side down on top of the first fabric and pin in place.

5 Turn stabilizer over and, from the back, stitch the line between shapes 1 and 2. Turn to front, press gently.

6 Bend stabilizer along the next line to be sewn and trim any excess fabric to leave a ¼" (7.5 mm) seam allowance. Press gently. Line up piece number 3 along the trimmed edge, pin, and sew as before.

7 Continue to sew the patches in numbered order onto the stabilizer until the block is complete.

8 Press the finished block and trim as necessary.

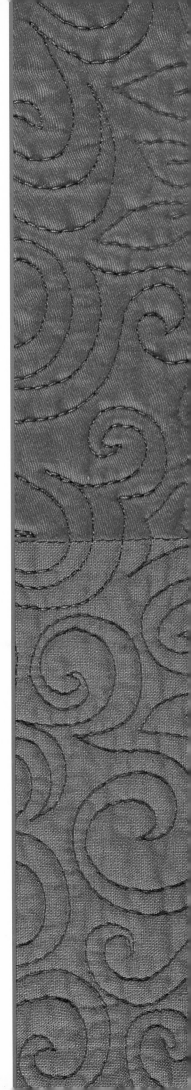

QUILTING

For many, the quilting stitch is somewhat of an afterthought as all the emphasis is placed onto the appliqué or patchwork. But for others, stitching the quilting pattern is the main focus of the quilt. In recent years the development of long-arm quilting machines has renewed interest in all-over quilting designs. Many commercial patterns are now available. Flower and leaf motifs are ideal for quilting because their organic shapes make them fun to stitch and easy to use in a variety of styles.

DAISY DOODLE STRIPPY
Ingrid Press
East Sussex, England
2003
48 × 38½" (122 × 98 cm)

Strippy quilts don't come much more contemporary than this tomato red and deep lime five-strip reversible quilt. The complementary colors produce an effect called simultaneous contrast in which they appear to vibrate. The machine quilting doodles over the whole surface of the quilt irrespective of the strip seams. Ingrid has incorporated a wide variety of flower motifs, ferns, and leaves. Two colors of quilting thread were used, and the quilting designs appear and disappear, depending on which color strip they are in.

**DAISY DOODLE
STRIPPY**

Ingrid Press
East Sussex, England
2003
48 × 38½"
(122 × 98 cm)

THE QUILTING STITCH IS MUCH MORE than a method of securing layers of fabric and batting (wadding). The pattern provides a complementary and supportive design element, reinforcing the impact of any appliqué and pieced designs. Alternatively, the quilting can deliberately act as a contrast that provides some tension in the finished work and prevents the quilt from being predictable.

The different styles of quilting, such as wholecloth, strippy, trapunto, free-style machining, and long-arm quilting, all have different characteristics that can be exploited to suit an individual quilt. Other factors include batting (wadding) types and thread qualities, both of which can be used in different combinations for particular effects.

ENGLISH DAFFODIL

Jayne Hill
Hampshire, England
2001
39½ × 39½"
(100 × 100 cm)

This is an interesting example of a wholecloth quilt whose design is based on an appliqué pattern, Edyth Henry's *Hawaiian Daffodil* (page 41), which was given to Jane as a wedding present. This was quilted on a long-arm machine with additional trapunto quilting that helps define the eight interlocking daffodils.

MACHINE QUILTING

In the past decade, the growth in popularity of long-arm quilting machines has been remarkable. In the United States alone, there are thousands of machines in use by both amateur and professional quilters. Long-arm machines are handguided and run on a track system or occasionally a suspended frame. They are not automated and require skillful operation to stitch evenly across the entire surface of a quilt. The major difference between quilting on a long-arm machine and a traditional sewing machine is that all the quilting is done from one side of the quilt to the other. The quilt top, batting (wadding), and backing are stretched onto canvas rollers. This means that the pattern must be broken into linear sections as the parts of the quilt top not being quilted are eased onto the rollers.

WHOLECLOTH AND STRIPPY QUILTS

This quilt features ornate designs across the entire surface, uninterrupted by piecing or appliqué. In the nineteenth and early twentieth centuries the style was particularly common in Wales and in the northeast England in the the counties of Northumberland and Durham. The quilts provided a showcase for the quilters' skills.

WHITE FLORAL BASKET

Cornelia Thompson Noyes

New York, USA

1852–53

99 × 83"

(251 × 211 cm)

This quilt features a wealth of floral motifs, starting with a trellis basket at the center from which four fragile flowers are growing. Two leaf vines echo the geometric shapes found in Oriental carpets. As is common with Baltimore Album quilts, botanical accuracy has been forsaken. Several different species seem to grow from the same stem.

Shelburne Museum

Strippy quilts, as their name suggests, are sewn from an odd number of fabric strips, usually five, seven, or nine, stretching from top to bottom. The colors can contrast greatly, such as Turkey red and white. The strips can be in plain or patterned fabrics or a combination.

Traditionally, wholecloth and strippy quilts were quilted by hand. In recent years, machine quilting has become more popular. Also, it has gained acceptance at major quilting exhibitions and competitions as an equal skill to hand quilting. As a result, wholecloth quilts have found new fans among machine quilters. Long-arm quilting machines in particular have increased the possibilities for machine stitchers. Their hand guided operation and ease of movement across the surface of the quilt are ideally suited for quilting wholecloths.

In the mid-nineteenth century bleached, machine woven cotton became readily available in the United States. Wholecloth quilts, also called white work, made use of this fabric and responded to a fashion trend for white bedrooms. Some of these quilts featured trapunto quilting and mimicked Boutis quilting from France, which uses cording to add texture.

Appliqué motifs can be used as quilting designs and vice versa, as illustrated by the quilts, *Two's Tulips* (page 92) and *Rose of Sharon* (page 97). By repeating the same pattern, greater impact is given to the design. Also by varying techniques, the quilter can call attention to different aspects of the designs.

WHOLECLOTH QUILT

The Murray Family
Northumberland,
England
c. 1850
101 × 97"
(256 × 246 cm)

This quilt was supposedly sewn by members of the Murray family in Allendale, an area of Northumberland known for wholecloth quilting. The cotton quilt features a large flower basket at the center with borders of oval leaves, and a hammock and daisy border pattern.
Bowes Museum

HOMESPUN WOOL QUILT
Member of the
Keith Family
Northumberland,
England
1875–1900
87 × 68"
(220 × 172 cm)

The homespun wool in this quilt was probably mill-woven and the top fabric is hand-dyed. The quilting design follows a seven-column strip format, unusual for a wholecloth quilt. Alternate stripes of wavy lines and a diamond filler pattern are interspersed with roses and four-petalled flower motifs.
Bowes Museum

QUILTING MOTIFS AND BATTING (WADDING)

When quilting stitches are sewn close together in a quilt, they flatten the surface. Areas left unquilted appear raised in contrast. By using a combination of densely and sparsely quilted motifs, the quilt design has more interesting definition, and better use of light and shadow.

For a main design on an appliqué quilt, consider any applied motifs that could be interpreted in stitching only. (Look at the *Rose of Sharon* project on page 97 as an example).

Tulips and daisies are particularly good to copy, and sprays of leaves can float around the appliqué. The patterns do not need to match exactly. An example of this is a sunflower appliqué, which could be quilted with flowers with only eight petals or with a wreath whose feathers give the impression of a multi-petalled flower. Contour or outline quilting is another option around appliqué designs and is a good choice for a beginner. Simply echo the outline of the flowers and leaves in increments of about ¼–½ inch (0.6 –1.3 cm).

When quilting a pieced quilt top, there are two opposing schools of thought. If you have a block with angles, reinforce this image with straight line quilting. If the piecing is curved, echo this with curved quilting lines. However, another approach is to do the opposite, using curved quilting patterns with straight piecing. Such a contrast can be very effective.

Filler patterns are small repeating patterns, such as crosshatching (a diamond pattern), tramlines (parallel lines), or meander (stipple) quilting. These are useful for filling in areas not quilted with a larger pattern. If the quilt features a very elaborate design, filler patterns may be the best option; so the quilting does not compete with the appliqué or patchwork.

The type of batting (wadding) can also affect the finished appearance of the quilt. Synthetic and natural battings have higher or lower loft properties and also require quilting stitches at different intervals. For a flat "antique" look, cotton batting is the best choice, although quilting

TWO'S TULIPS
Sandie Lush
Bristol, England
2000
42 × 32"
(107 × 81 cm)

The quilt features a version of an original wholecloth pattern designed by Sandie and Barbara Chainey, both well-known, expert hand quilters. The tulip quilting design was converted to appliqué and attached using freezer paper to show how interchangeable floral patterns can be. The mirror-image layout and pastel color scheme create a calm and pleasing quilt.

FUCHSIARAMA

Maureen Baker

Essex, England

2000

90 × 75"

(229 × 191 cm)

This incredible hand-stitched wholecloth won first prize at Quilts UK in 2001. The original design has an excellent balance of elements—central motifs, elaborate border designs, and filler patterns. Fuchsias are a favorite flower for Maureen and inspired the startling color scheme. Drooping bell-shaped flowers are featured in the wide border and corners and are stitched with embroidery thread in a back stitch. Trapunto work adds dramatic emphasis.

patterns are less visible. Polyester battings generally give a puffier appearance because of their higher loft. Wool batting (wadding) acts more like polyester in its loft properties although it produces a much warmer quilt.

Generally, if the quilt is divided into blocks they can be marked with the quilting pattern one at a time. For a hand-quilted wholecloth,

the entire quilt top is marked before stitching. For machine quilting, the top is marked beforehand unless the quilting is to be freehand. Another exception is long-arm quilting. With this technique the purchased quilting patterns are laid flat next to the machine and the design is traced manually by a laser or metal stylus. When a pieced or appliquéd

**WHIG ROSE
VARIATION**

Maker unknown
Possibly Ohio, USA
c. 1850
98 × 77"
(249 × 196 cm)

Compare this quilt with
the one on page 31 for
similarities in the design
of the appliqué block.
The diagonal layout of
the Turkey red and pink
flower sprays forms an
eye-pleasing trellis
pattern. The plain blocks
have sumptuous hand
quilting and trapunto
work featuring full-
blown roses and flower
buds. In contrast to the
expertly planned center,
the rose vine border has
a more random
approach with its
multiple blooms
disappearing off the
edges of the quilt in the
top two corners.
University of Nebraska-
Lincoln

quilt top features a plain fabric on the reverse, the bonus is often a wholecloth quilt for no extra effort. However, occasionally such precise quilting can backfire. When Jayne Hill's attractive pieced quilt *Labour of Love* (page 95) was proudly shown to her husband Max, he promptly turned it over. The plain muslin (calico) back shows the quilting extremely well. Max's comment was, "It's lovely, but I do wish you'd make a wholecloth. All that piecing detracts from the quilting."

REDWORK STITCHING

Redwork quilts first appeared in Europe in the early nineteenth century and were in their heyday in the Victorian era when girls were encouraged to practice their embroidery skills on plain squares of material. The squares were preprinted with a

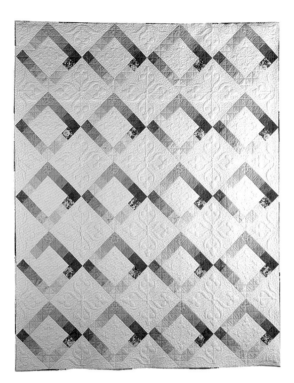

variety of designs (including those by illustrator Kate Greenaway) and were sold for a penny. The resulting quilts are also called Penny Quilts. From 1850 this form of outline embroidery became known as Turkey work. As the name suggests, they were often stitched in thread dyed in color-fast Turkey red on white backgrounds. The same style was sewn in white thread on red and arranged checkerboard style. The designs were traced onto heavy paper with holes pierced at regular intervals to mark the outlines. Quilt-makers used a variety of substances to dab through the holes and mark the dotted pattern on the fabric.

In the twentieth century, redwork patterns by quilt designers such as Ruby Short McKim were syndicated in newspapers and published by companies such as Vogue. Floral designs, urns, and baskets were often featured alongside whimsical designs of animals, alphabets, children, and Sunbonnet Sue characters. One of McKim's redwork designs from 1932 features a 48-block quilt of the state flowers of each American state. Because these squares were stitched, the floral designs could be lifelike, much like botanical drawings. At this time, there was also a fashion for Dutch-inspired quilts, so redwork designs can also be found stitched in blue. These are known as blue redwork!

Redwork squares were also made for Album quilts, since their light and airy designs left plenty of space for an embroidered signature. A variety of different embroidery stitches can be used. Common stitches include French knots, double chain stitch, stem stitch, satin stitch and lazy daisy stitch. Further decorative embroidery was used on the seamlines of the blocks. In the past decade there has been renewed interest in redwork because of books published by Betty Alderman, Alex Anderson, and Deborah Harding promoting this method. Nevertheless, most quilts are still quite traditional in terms of the images chosen for stitching.

TRAPUNTO QUILTING

Also known as stuffed quilting, this technique creates areas with greater definition. It is ideal for emphasising quilted flowers, baskets, bouquets, berries, and leaves. In the area to be stuffed, the outline is stitched first to prevent extra batting from shifting around the quilt. Working from the back of the quilt, ease the threads of the backing fabric apart to make a small hole and insert extra batting, using a crochet hook. After stuffing, the threads are eased back into place. For large sections of trapunto, it may be necessary to cut a small slit in the backing fabric to add the batting.

LABOUR OF LOVE
Jayne Hill
Hampshire, England
2001
80 × 68"
(203 × 173 cm)

FRUITS OF THE FOREST
Jayne Hill
Hampshire, England
2002
58 × 58"
(147 × 147 cm)

In the *Mexican Rose* quilt project (page 103) trapunto has been used to raise areas on individual petals and flower centers.

For a similar effect, leave parts unquilted or quilt around appliqué motifs. If you are using a polyester batting (wadding) with a higher loft, the unquilted areas will appear puffier. However, be careful that these areas do not sag. One solution is to quilt around the motifs exactly on the seam line.

GRAPE IN AUTUMN

Eiko Okano and
Hisae Machiaoka
Tokyo, Japan
2000
75 × 71"
(190 × 180 cm)

This marvellous quilt was a collaboration between Eiko Okano as designer and Hisae Machiaoka as quiltmaker. The grape vines are appliquéd with trapunto stuffing, and the hand quilted trellis basket at the center features daisies, roses, and cascading ferns leaves. The quilting clearly shows how a combination of main, border, and filler patterns combines to produce a modern heirloom.

TECHNIQUE
HAND QUILTING
INSPIRED BY THE QUILT: ROSE OF SHARON

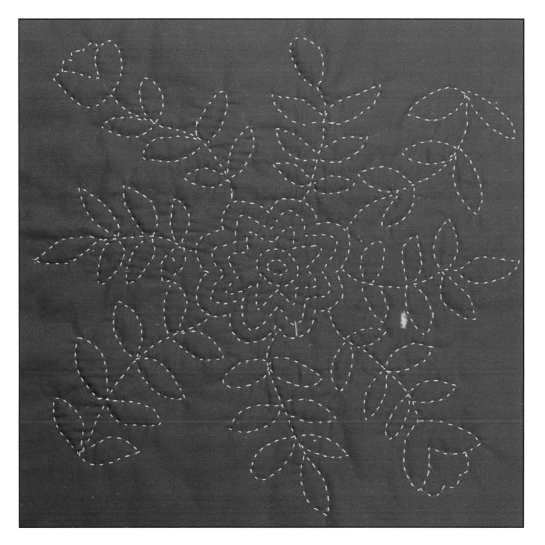

ROSE OF SHARON

Unknown quiltmaker, possibly Pennsylvania, USA

85 × 84" (216 × 213 cm), c. 1870

The Rose of Sharon is a variation of the Whig Rose design (page 94). The name refers to the Song of Solomon, a love poem from the Old Testament. It was one of the most popular floral patterns throughout the nineteenth century and because of its religious inspiration was a favorite for quilts made for ministers or for fundraising.

University of Nebraska-Lincoln

Quiltmakers can look beyond existing quilting patterns when they are seeking inspiration for quilting designs. The boldness of the Rose of Sharon appliqué makes it ideal for translation into a handquilting design. Simply extract the parts of the pattern that appeal and adapt as necessary—such as here where the central flower design has concentric rows of quilting to fill the large space. This makes a superb quilting pattern to add interest in plain setting squares and to complement an appliqué block design. A lightbox has been used to trace the pattern, but an alternative is to photocopy the design and tape it and the fabric against a window.

MATERIALS FOR ONE BLOCK

- 13½ × 13½" (34 × 34 cm)
  red cotton fabric
- 15 × 15" (38 × 38 cm) cotton batting (wadding)
- 15½ × 15½" (40 × 40 cm) neutral-colored cotton backing fabric
- Light-colored watercolor or quilt marking pencil
- Lightbox
- Basting (tacking) thread
- Cream quilting thread
- Pins
- Needle
- Thimble
- Fabric scissors

1 For dark fabrics, place the pattern from page 148 on a lightbox. Place fabric on top of pattern and trace through, using a quilt marking pencil. For pale fabrics, it may be possible to trace the design without additional light.

2 Layer the top fabric, batting (wadding) and backing fabric and pin. Baste (tack) starting with two lines crossing through the center and work toward the outsides. As these stitches will be removed later, keep the knots on the top of the fabric.

3 Cut a length of quilting thread no longer than 18" (45 cm) and start to quilt from the center. The central flower has the outline and center circle marked. Fill in the rest of the flower as you wish. Concentrate on using even running stitches of equal size rather than the tiniest stitch possible! When you are stitching the stems and leaves, stitch from the center toward the end leaf. The intermediate leaves can then be stitched in order.

4 Remove the basting (tacking) when all the quilting is done. It is a good idea to keep the outer line of basting (tacking) in place until the pieces are sewn together so they remain square.

TECHNIQUE
HAND APPLIQUÉ
INSPIRED BY THE QUILT: THE DAISY QUILT

THE DAISY QUILT
Philippa Naylor
Dhahran, Saudi Arabia
2001
59 × 47½" (149 × 121 cm)

Philippa started with sketches of daisies because she wanted the flowers to be stylized yet true to nature. Each petal was fused to interfacing and appliquéd by hand onto the background. The variety of blue fabrics (many hand-dyed) ensures that the daisies contrast well. Trapunto quilted daisy flower heads and stems add depth to the design. The rest of the quilt is covered in free motion machine quilting using a vermicelli pattern.

This quilt was awarded first prize for Amateur Quilts and the Quilters' Guild Workmanship award at the National Quilt Championships, UK, 2001.

Although daisies are a well-known garden flower in Western Europe and USA, this member of the chrysanthemum family is actually a native of China and southern Japan where it was already in cultivation by 500 BC. Its simple shape is easy to interpret in appliqué and quilting, and so it is a flower often used on quilts (see also Indian Daisy on page 37 and Daisy Daisy on page 38).

Note: This project shows you how to appliqué the daisy motif. However, you could also combine this pattern with plain blocks set on point and use the appliqué design as a pattern for hand or machine quilting on these plain blocks.

MATERIALS FOR ONE BLOCK

- Pencil
- Paper
- Tracing paper
- Blue fabric for backing
- Green fabric for stem
- Orange fabric for daisy
- Brown fabric for daisy center
- Basting (tacking) thread
- Green, orange and brown thread
- Sewing machine (optional)
- Brown embroidery floss for French knots

1 Using the template on page 147, trace the pattern on tracing paper using a pencil and a light box. Retrace the design onto the wrong sides of the background fabric and number the parts.

2 From the wrong side of the background fabric baste (tack) through the fabric so the stem is outlined.

3 Cut a bias strip 1¼" (3⅓ cm) wide. Press in half lengthways, then fold the raw edges two-thirds of the way under the strip.

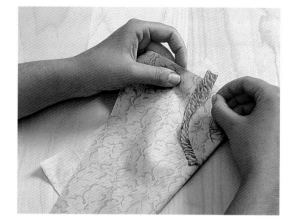

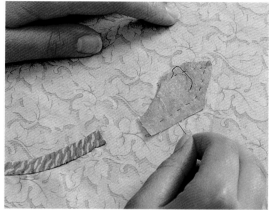

4 Pin in place. Stitch down, using either a hand needle and a small slipstitch (blind stitch) or by machine set for narrow satin stitch. The threads should match the color of the fabric being sewn.

5 Cut a shape that is larger than the first petal. Lay this on the background. With the light behind the fabric check the placement of the petal. There should be at least least ¼" (6 mm) overhanging the lines. Cut away any excess fabric. Baste (tack) through on pencil lines on the reverse. Removing a small amount of the basting (tacking) thread at a time, slipstitch (blind stitch) the petal down. It is not necessary to stitch where the next pattern piece will overlap.

6 Continue until all the petals are sewn in place.

7 Trace the center of the flower onto a scrap of card. Cut a piece of dark fabric ¼" (6 mm) larger than the card. Stitch a gathering thread at the edge of the fabric, place the card at the center and gather the fabric round it. Iron the gathers and, when the fabric has cooled down, gently ease the card out. Pin the fabric center in place and stitch round. French knots may be added with embroidery floss.

TECHNIQUE
MACHINE TRAPUNTO
INSPIRED BY THE QUILT: MEXICAN ROSE

MEXICAN ROSE

Maker unknown, probably Pennsylvania, USA, c. 1880

94 × 92" (239 × 234 cm)

The dramatic color scheme in this nineteenth century quilt is typical of Pennsylvanian Dutch quilts which favored yellow backgrounds. The shape of the petals gives an energy to the quilt as if the flower heads are swaying in the wind. The yellow applique blocks are balanced by the wide border of the same color featuring an undulating vine of rose buds and open flowers. Fine hand quilting decorates the entire quilt surface—the red blocks feature quilted bouquets and the rest of the quilt is covered by diamond crosshatching.

University of Nebraska-Lincoln

Trapunto (also known as stuffed quilting) is ideal for adding emphasis to certain parts of an appliqué design or a whole-cloth quilt. Unlike quilting whose function is to hold the layers securely in place, trapunto is purely decorative. Depending on the areas to be stuffed, the padding may be done before the motif is applied or afterwards, in which case the extra batting is inserted from the reverse of the fabric. The quilt top is then layered with batting (wadding) and a backing fabric and quilted as normal. The effects of trapunto are more clearly seen on solid-color fabrics because an obvious shadow is created by the extra padding.

1 Trace the templates (page 149) onto the right side of the background fabric with fine light pencil.

MATERIALS FOR ONE BLOCK
- 10 × 8" (25 × 20 cm) yellow cotton
- 10 × 8" (25 × 20 cm) red cotton
- 3 × 3" (8 × 8 cm) orange cotton
- 1 × 2" (2½ × 5 cm) black cotton
- Matching threads
- Fabric pencil
- Scrap of card
- Small amount of batting (wadding)
- Small wooden stick to pull wool through
- Needle
- Scissors
- Sewing machine

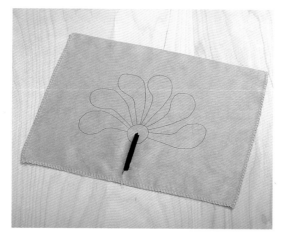

2 Fold under ¼" (6 mm) at each long side of the black fabric strip. Position one edge where the stem will lie, and stitch the folded edge down. Ease other side of stem slightly closer to the first edge and stitch so that a little fullness is left in the stem fabric.

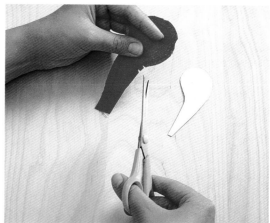

3 Make a card template of the petal. Trace around the template on the wrong side of the red fabric. Machine stitch just outside the pencil line using matching thread. Trim outer edge to ¼" (6 mm) outside the stitched line and clip the curved edge.

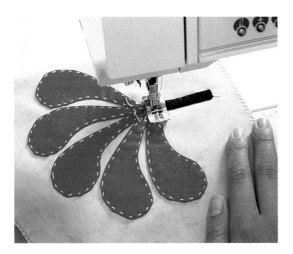

4 Turn under the raw edge at the stitched line and baste (tack) to background. Set the machine to a shorter stitch length and width and machine appliqué the petals in place using a slipstitch (blind stitch).

5 Cut a 1¾" (4½ cm) circle of orange fabric for the flower center. Stitch just inside the outer edge with running stitch. Pull up the threads to gather, stuff lightly, then pull closed. Stitch in place with slipstitch (blind stitch).

6 Turn the block to the wrong side and from the back make a small hole behind the petal by separating the warp and weft threads. Lightly stuff the petals through the hole, using the wood stick. Poke the batting (wadding) to all parts of the petal. Close the opening and repeat with the other petals.

The finished blocks are left unpressed.

FLORAL
BORDERS

Although sometimes given little thought, the border is an essential element of a quilt's design. For quilts that have a more traditional appearance, a border offers the final opportunity to frame a quilt. A successful border can transform an ordinary repeating block pattern into a unique design where all the elements work together. Contemporary quilters may decide to omit a four-sided border if their design occupies the total surface. Alternatively, borders can be asymmetric or on two sides. Floral vines are often used for quilt borders, but look closely at the quilts in this book for many more ideas.

GARDEN WREATH

Maker unknown

USA

Nineteenth century

87 × 71" (221 × 180 cm)

In this jazzy quilt, the border is as important as the central blocks. This equality is achieved by the boldness of the Wandering Tulip vine pattern and the careful choice of colors. The bold green, red, and white color scheme is the same as in the 12 floral blocks, which feature an assortment of pieced and appliqué designs such as Carolina Lily, Rose Wreath, and Christmas Cactus, thus achieving a balance to the colorful quilt center.

The American Museum in Britain

ALMOST CREWEL

Marilyn Badger

Oregon, USA

1999

100 × 84"

(254 × 213 cm)

The central panel in this exquisitely appliquéd quilt is set off by complementary borders. The floral patterns, adapted from designs by Betty Cossey, were hand-appliquéd. The subtle Bali prints and Marilyn's own hand-dyed fabrics in the petals and leaves add interest to this airy design. *Almost Crewel* was awarded first prize for Heirloom Quilting at Machine Quilters Showcase, USA, 2000.

TO ACHIEVE SUCCESSFUL FLORAL borders, a quilter must consider various factors when designing the quilt. These include format, complexity of pattern and its relation to the central design, the role of the border in the overall design, and whether to finalize the design at the initial planning stage or leave a degree of flexibility for adjustments or design changes when the border is added later.

FORMATS

Just as there are an infinite number of quilt top patterns, border formats are equally flexible. Regardless of the pattern chosen, the first decision must be the number and position of the borders. The most commonly used style is four borders of equal width surrounding the central pattern (see Garden Wreath, page 107). One variation is to sew borders on three sides (usually not the top,

**STARFLOWER
GARDEN**
Margaret Docherty
Durham, England
1998
81 × 68½"
(206 × 174 cm)

A deep blue border in
which 24 pieced
starflowers seem to
dance on their
appliquéd stems makes
a beautiful frame for this
quilt. A subtle color
gradation on the petals
and leaves echoes the
changing color of the
center blocks. The
border features
trapunto as well as hand
quilting.

which is tucked in at the top of the bed). Or the borders can vary in width. Usually the top and bottom are equal. This is helpful to size the central design to a specific measurement. If the variation is only one or two inches (up to 5 cm), the variation may not even be noticeable in the final quilt. Marilyn Badger's quilt *Almost Crewel* on page 108 shows another option. The top border is wider than the others, and the appliqué has been adjusted to a more open pattern to make use of the extra space.

Another variations is to use cornerstones, or squares, at the corners. This arrangement can provide a pleasing, balanced effect, especially when the cornerstone fabrics echo the central design. *Heavenly Flowers* by Noriko Haba (page 110) is a good example of this apparent mirror imagery. However, if you look closely, you realize that no designs are identical.

**HEAVENLY
FLOWERS**

Noriko Haba

Nara, Japan

1999

47 × 47"

(120 × 120 cm)

The use of mottled hand-dyed fabrics gives this quilt an ethereal quality. Delicate hand-appliquéd flowers entwine with ribbons and birds in the central panel. The darker blue borders and black printed binding provide an excellent balance of color to the center. The imagery in the borders and corner squares is different in each section, which prevents the design being predictable. The sympathetic color scheme produces a harmonious overall effect.

The number of borders used can also have an impact on the overall effect of the quilt. Generally when there are two or more borders, the quilt appears more sophisticated. Borders need not be of equal complexity. In fact, when one "key" border is given greater importance, more attention is drawn to the main pattern. In *Souvenir of Sulaiman* by Josephine Ratcliff, (right) the seven borders actually cover most of the surface area of the quilt.

In the 1920s, central floral designs surrounded by vines, sprays of flowers, and ribbons were popular. Scalloped edges were also common and complemented flowing border patterns. This tradition is carried on still by contemporary quilter Margaret Tashiro Caccamo. Her quilt *Grandfather's not Grandmother's Garden* is on page 22. In her book *Soft Covers for Hard Times,* Merikay Waldvogel suggests that such shaped edges quilts may have been popular because of the recent availability of machine-made bias tape.

For contemporary designs, borders might not be required. With pictorial quilts, the imagery may have been designed to fill the entire quilt surface and in this case a wide or fussy border would be detrimental to the overall design. *Poppy Field* by

Emily Parson, (page 7), is a good example of this. Emily has taken the poppy flowers and leaves right to (and beyond) the edge to produce great vitality, with flowers unconstrained by boundaries. Rather than having a border, great care has been taken with the binding; it is pieced so that it color coordinates with the quilt—another design trick which is useful to learn.

SOUVENIR OF SULAIMAN

Josephine Ratcliff
Lancashire, England
1994
94 × 67"
(239 × 170 cm)

Inspired by Islamic ceramic tiles at the Victoria & Albert Museum in London, this quilt was sewn using reverse appliqué. The magnificent border features the subtly changing blues and violets in morning glory flowers (convolvulus). All the borders have mitered corners, ensuring that the pattern fabric flows smoothly around the corners.

Borders may be part of the overall quilt layout but they need not be symmetrical or even obvious as borders. *Indian Daisy* by Ingrid Press (page 37) illustrates this tactic. Ingrid has taken the idea of flexible borders to the extreme. The main image is surrounded on all sides by up to four borders which are pieced and quilted. Because of the varying widths of the framing strips, the central image is not in the middle of the quilt. Nevertheless, the repetition of imagery and colors results in a quilt that is balanced and visually appealing.

BORDER PATTERNS

Appliquéd bouquets, urns, and blooms can naturally cascade into vines of flower and leaves or individual blooms entwining the border strips. Pieced patterns can be more difficult to interpret for borders. However, one possibility is to sew a Sawtooth (triangle) pattern or Flying Geese block that

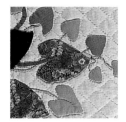

CONVOLVULUS
Carol Boyce
Monmouthshire, Wales
1986
72 × 72"
(183 × 183 cm)

The work of Arts and Crafts designer William Morris provided the original inspiration. The way in which the plants seem to grow over the border and central circle gives life to what could have been a rather formal layout. The quilt is hand appliquéd and quilted with additional embroidered stems and French knots on the flowers.

uses the fabrics in the main body of the quilt (see *Flowers in the Cabin* by Pam Clarke, page 70). If squares are used in the block, another option is to piece squares set on point to give the appearance of the Diamond in the Square block. Florence Peto has used this idea for her quilt *Calico Garden* (page 71) where the border squares echo the nine-patch blocks at the center.

If the central design of the quilt is very complex, there are two options when designing the outer edges. A simple border may be required to "calm down" the overall appearance of the quilt. In this case, the border acts as a frame and must have enough weight to balance the central pattern. This can be achieved by using both dark and light fabrics. Colors should be chosen carefully to ensure that there is still some cohesion. One solution is to have a wide border with an inner border or binding in a brighter color directly linked to the main design. *Where Have all the Flowers Gone?* by Norma Bassett (page 26) uses this technique with black fabric. Another variation is to have two wide borders but use the darker color as the inner frame so that the outer border balances the center.

Nineteenth-century quilters seem to be fond of the "more is better" outlook. Exuberant

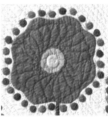

POTS OF FLOWERS
Maker unknown
Possibly Ohio, USA
c. 1860–1880
81½ × 80½"
(207 × 204 cm)

Despite the simple appearance of this four-block pattern, the maker of this quilt was highly skilled. There are more than 2,600 small appliquéd circles around the flower heads and on the stems. Dense diagonal quilting interspersed with sunflower-type patterns and a red piping add the final details to an extraordinary quilt.
University of Nebraska-Lincoln

WHIG ROSE
Maker unknown
Possibly Indiana, USA
c. 1850–1860
92 × 94"
(234 × 239 cm)

The border design is astounding for this bold nine-block quilt. A complex pattern of interlinking floral vines and bunches of grapes is separated by four urns filled with roses and tulips. Fine hand quilting covers the surface with leaves and vines. This quilt is almost identical to another known to have been sewn in Ohio, so the design may have moved west with pioneers or been exchanged within a family.
University of Nebraska-Lincoln

appliqué designs often repeat blocks around the edge, resulting in busy floral quilts. *Pots of Flowers* (page 113) illustrates this approach. The large flower pattern has been reduced and used in the border design. The quiltmaker has carefully calculated the size of the motifs to fit the four sides. Single flowers heads fill the spaces at each corner.

Just as the size of the border strips can vary, so can the patterns. A successful border often contains the same elements or colors to provide a balanced structure, even if the actual patterns are different. *Wragg Time* by Mary Mayne (page 40) illustrates this approach. Mary's quilt actually follows the four borders and cornerstones layout, yet she has used a variety of pieced and appliquéd patterns.

Finally, an essential factor when planning a border is the ability of the pattern to fit the length of border or flow around the corners. For beginning quilters it may be best to choose borders with cornerstones or a design that stops short of the corners. Separate motifs can then be placed there. If planning a cascading vine, the pattern can be designed from the center of one side. At the corner, mirrors, photocopying, or scanning and flipping computer programs can be used to reverse the pattern and achieve a flow around corners. *Celebration*, Maureen Baker's quilt

INDIA

Christine Moulin
Soisy-sur-Seine, France
2002
41½ × 41½"
(105 × 105 cm)

While her daughter was spending two years with a humanitarian organization in India, Christine was inspired to sew this quilt. It is based on a pattern at the Taj Mahal and these words in the Koran: "Have no fear, remember the promised garden." This exquisite and unique floral quilt features appliqué, gold thread embroidery, and trapunto work in addition to dense machine quilting. The central flower design extends like a compass and is surrounded by a series of circular and trellis-like borders.

(page 14), demonstrates how a designed border adds a final flourish. The continuous grapevine used in the border is well designed for the space. The print uses the same shade of green from the blocks and inner sashing. This quilt is also an example of a quilter's lateral thinking: The purchased fabric turned out to be too harsh but the reverse of the material was perfect!

The border is your final opportunity to frame your floral quilt. There is no single right approach and patient planning is important. Waiting until the center of the quilt is finished may be the best idea. You can then assess the impact of any repeating patterns, color combinations, and secondary designs. With appliquéd or pieced borders, the relationship with the central design and how best to support it should be considered. For simpler borders sewn with solid color or patterned fabric, experiment with folded materials next to the quilt top to assess both the color and the width of the border.

TECHNIQUE
HAND PIECING
INSPIRED BY THE QUILT: DOREEN'S DUTCH TILES

DOREEN'S DUTCH TILES

Nancy Rink, California, USA, 2000

107 × 87" (272 × 221 cm)

This quilt contains a mix of European inspiration—a range of French style fabrics designed by the late quilter, Doreen Speckman, and a patchwork block that reminded Nancy of Dutch ceramic tiles. To expand the Dutch theme, appliqué tulips were added in each corner and the wandering vine border contains tulips. Hand appliqué and machine piecing and quilting produced this masterpiece, which was winner of two first prize awards at the Kern County Fair and the Best of the Valley quilt show, both in California, USA.

This bright and cheery quilt is an excellent example of how all the elements combine to produce a balanced design. The patchwork blocks are pieced in primary colors and surrounded by equally bold sashing. The appliqué vine border contains the same colors as the blocks but complements rather than competes with the geometric center. Nancy has carefully spaced the vine design using gentle curves and a simple repeat pattern. At the corners, the two vines meet in an arch. The rounded blue flower is a useful device linking the two stems, eliminating the need for the bias to curve sharply, which is difficult to achieve.

You can break the design into shorter pattern repeats and practice drawing the stem in a gentle curve. Photocopy the pattern to show the effect of the repeat. Trace a reverse and photocopy to see how the pattern works at each corner.

MATERIALS FOR ONE BLOCK

- 11 × 11" (28 × 28 cm) white cotton fabric
- 2 × 10" (5 × 25 cm) dark green cotton fabric
- 4 × 4" (10 × 10 cm) blue cotton fabric
- 4 × 4" (10 × 10 cm) yellow cotton fabric
- Scraps of green cotton for leaves
- Fine marking pencil
- Matching threads
- Basting (tacking) thread
- White card stock
- Spray starch
- Cotton buds
- Needle
- Scissors or rotary cutter and board

1 Use a lightbox and the template on page 149 to trace the design onto the background fabric.

2 Cut bias strips 1 × 10" (2½ × 25 cm) from the dark green fabric for the stems. Fold the edges to the middle and iron to make bias stems.

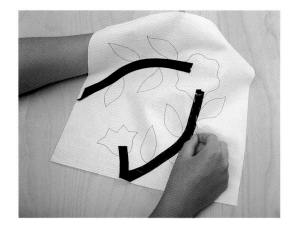

3 Baste (tack) the stems on to the background fabric, pulling gently to curve the bias strips. Stitch the inside curves first. Using matching thread, slipstitch (blind stitch) the stems in place, again sewing the inside curve first.

4 Cut templates for the leaves and flowers from the white card stock and mark the right and wrong sides. Place the reversed template on the wrong side of the fabric, and cut out with ¼" (6 mm) allowance. Spray a small amount of starch into a saucer. Dip a cotton ball into the starch and dab onto the turn line. With a hot iron, carefully press the fabric over the card, clipping curves. Remove the template and trim excess fabric if necessary.

5 Baste (tack) the leaves and flowers in place making sure they are evenly spaced. Slipstitch (blind stitch) using matching threads.

TECHNIQUE
HAND APPLIQUÉ
INSPIRED BY THE QUILT: COCKSCOMB AND TULIPS

COCKSCOMB AND TULIPS

Maker unknown, possibly Ohio, USA, c. 1850

96 × 96" (244 × 244 cm)

This quilt is a good example of borders being as important to the central design. Nine cockscomb blocks, set on point, are arranged in the middle of the quilt top. The style of the flowers and their size in comparison with the flowerpots creates a simple folk-art effect. An inner pieced sawtooth border crisply delineates the center, and a bold, graphic tulip vine twists around the outer border. The only deviation from all this meticulous sewing is the appliquéd outer sawtooth border where the corner triangles have been adjusted to fit the space available.

University of Nebraska-Lincoln

One of the challenges facing a quilter designing a border is how to tackle the movement of the pattern around the corners. While many quilts feature four identical corner treatments, the unknown quilter sewing this quilt opted for two solutions. Two opposing corners feature a deep curve enclosing one of the tulip flowers. The other two corners have a very gentle curve and two flowers growing from the same stem. Because the overall design is balanced symmetrically the difference in the design is not apparent at first glance. This tulip project has been sewn with a needleturn appliqué technique.

MATERIALS FOR ONE BLOCK

- 16 × 14" (40 × 35½ cm) background fabric
- 16 × 14" (40 × 35½ cm) black fabric for stems, leaves and sawtooth border
- Scrap of red fabric for tulips
- Medium pencil
- 16 × 14" (40 × 35½ cm) freezer paper
- Iron
- Pins
- Matching threads

1 Using a lightbox, lightly trace the pattern from page 150 onto the right side of the background fabric with a sharp medium pencil.
Trace the leaves, petals, and sawtooth edging onto the dull side of freezer paper.

2 Cut out the freezer paper templates and iron onto the right side of the black and red fabrics, leaving enough space all around the shapes for a ⅛" (3 mm) seam allowance.

3 Cut a 1" (2½ cm) wide bias strip from black fabric. Fold lengthways in half and press.

4 Place the cut edge of the bias strips against the pencil line on the background fabric. Pin and stitch in place by hand or machine about ⅛" (3 mm) from the cut edge. When in place, the folded edge of the long bias vine covers the cut edge of the stem. Pin and stitch as before, using matching threads.

5 Position the red petals and baste (tack) in place ¼" (7 mm) away from the edge. Slipstitch (blind stitch) the top edge of the petals and a little way down the sides, turning in a small seam allowance and snipping the inner angles. Do not stitch the lower edge.

6 Baste (tack), then slipstitch (blind stitch) the remaining black petals in place on top of the tulips. Next, baste and sew the leaves in place. Finally, baste and stitch the sawtooth edge in position, clipping the inner angles and crisply folding the seam allowance at the top of each triangle. Remove all basting threads and press from the reverse.

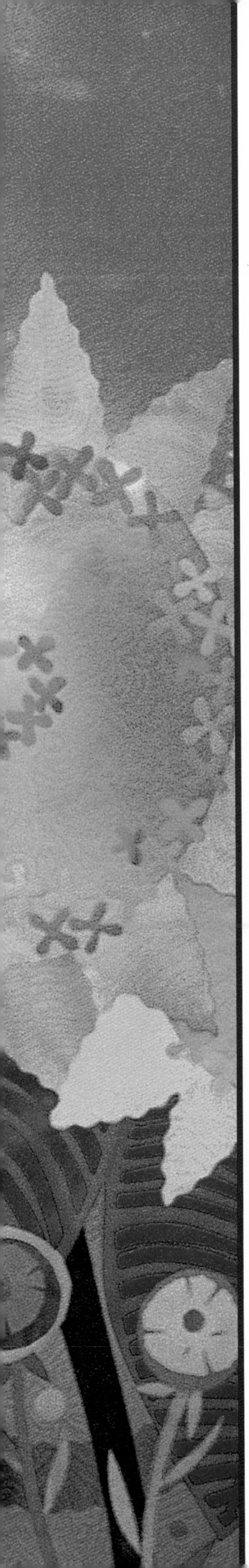

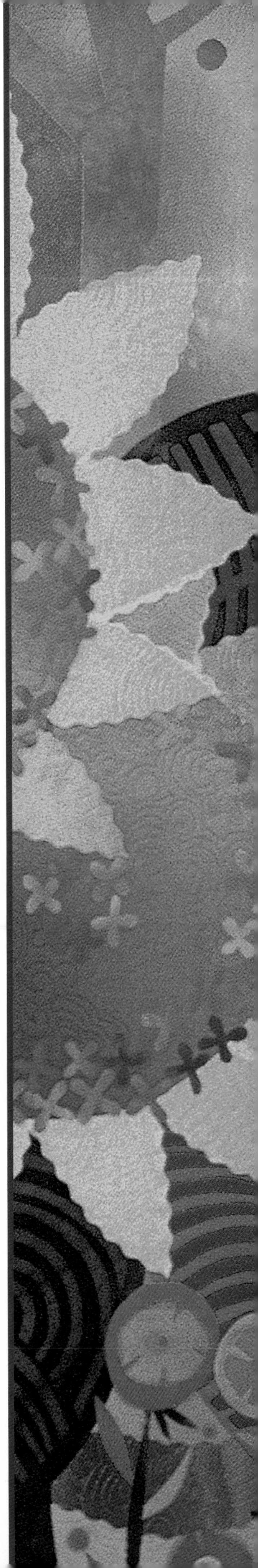

EMBELLISHED QUILTS

*For many quilt artists, embellished and hand colored quilts offer the ultimate freedom of expression. Quilters can experiment with a variety of techniques, whether hand or machine, painting or printing, embroidery or embellishment.
The resulting floral quilts can achieve realism much like textile photographs, or they can remain abstract expressions of the glory of flowers.
In twenty-first-century quiltmaking, anything goes!*

SUNFLOWERS #2

Melody Johnson

Illinois, USA

2002

19 × 26"

(48½ × 65½ cm)

Melody trained as an artist, and her quilt ideas often come from pencil sketches that she enlarges and refines in the design process. She started a fabric dyeing business in 1989 and included her hand-dyed cottons in this fantasy floral collage, which also features intensive surface decoration by machine stitching. This exuberant quilt was awarded two first prizes at the International Quilt Festival, USA, 2001, and at the American Quilter's Society show, 2002.

SNEEZEWEED

Melody Johnson

Illinois, USA

2000

13 × 13½"

(33 × 34 cm)

For this charming quilt, the hand-dyed fabrics were pressed onto fusible adhesive (bonding agent) before being cut and placed in position. The bright blue border acts as an effective frame for the composition. Machine and hand quilting secures the appliqué motifs in place. This is one of a series of quilts based on fantasy flowers. They provided a challenge for Melody who was not used to making pictorial quilts (but is now a convert!).

TODAY, MANY QUILTERS HAVE THE skills to color their own fabric through dyeing, printing, and painting. This enables them to create individual pieces of contemporary textile art. Another factor contributing to the freedom in quiltmaking is that the craft now embraces makers with a wide variety of design education backgrounds. Painters, embroiderers, and textile artists have all found that quilts offer a medium for their self-expression, whether abstract or literal. Finally, in Britain, education programs such as City & Guilds and the Diploma in Stitched Textiles have helped to broaden the technical skills base and design awareness for many previously traditional quiltmakers. This allows them to experiment in moving the quilting arts forward for a new century of creativity.

Embellishment allows quiltmakers the opportunity to use many techniques. For some, like American quilt artist Melody Johnson, design is paramount over technique. Whatever means are required to achieve an end result are viewed as acceptable, regardless of whether or not they are traditional to quiltmaking.

Embellishment is particularly suited to floral quilts because it enables details to be added to the pieced, painted, or appliquéd imagery. Colors can be made to merge as they do in nature. In particular, embroidery is especially good when a realistic impression of a flower head is desired. However, when deciding to add extra stitching, texture, or color on fabric, restraint must also be exercised. The intention of embellishment is to add interest to the original concept that is in keeping with it.

The additional techniques should contribute to the quilt imagery or pattern, yet not overwhelm it.

There are no set rules when it comes to embellishment. Embroiderers can choose hand-sewn embroidery stitches, whereas a machine quilter may concentrate on using the machine and free-stitching techniques. Thread choices can also be varied, whether one decides to use space-dyed cotton thread, shiny rayons and metallics, or thicker button thread and fancy yarns. Thick or slippery threads are usually wound

IN PRAISE OF POPPIES
Emilie M Belak
British Columbia, Canada
1995
57 × 47½"
(145 × 121 cm)

This is an extraordinary quilt with a wealth of attention to detail. Emilie developed the idea over two years and hand-painted fabrics when she realized commercial materials were not suitable. Machine embroidery on each leaf, petal, and seed head gives great depth to this machine appliquéd quilt, further enhanced by the three-dimensional petals. It was selected as one of the Twentieth Century's 100 Best American Quilts.

NOCTURNAL GARDEN

Ted Storm-van Weelden
s'Gravenzande,
The Netherlands
1997–2001
80 × 80"
(203 × 203 cm)

This dramatic quilt was inspired by a china pattern made by De Porceleyne Fles in Delft. The first impression is of the vivid color contrasts created by the black background and the powerful design layout. Closer inspection reveals the wealth of techniques used—hand and padded appliqué, hand embroidery, beading, shisha mirrors, padded trapunto, and hand quilting. The quilt was awarded Best of Show at the 2001 International Quilt Festival, Houston, USA.

onto the bobbin for machine sewing machine and sewn from the reverse of the quilt. This reduces the tension on the yarn, which is often the cause of broken threads.

PAINTED AND PRINTED QUILTS

By painting, dyeing, or printing a plain fabric, quilters have discovered the ultimate way to create one-of-a-kind pieces that are personal to the maker. To produce such fabrics, quilters have needed to learn other skills. As a result, quiltmaking has become more closely allied with other media, such as collage, embroidery, fine art textiles, felt, and papermaking.

Color can be applied to fabric in a number of ways. Dyeing of small pieces can be done in plastic bags, a jar, or the microwave. Alternatively, larger pieces can be dyed in a dye bath or washing machine. The colors may be subtle or bright, depending on the dyes and paints and concentration of the dye. Synthetic reactive powder dyes are most common and can be mixed to provide a variety of hues. They offer excellent depth of tone and color-fastness. For dyeing on a small scale, specialty hobby companies now manufacture a wide range of dyes suitable for coloring cotton, silk, and wool fabrics.

In addition to dyeing, small patches or appliqué motifs can be painted or colorwashed for specific effects or the edge of the fabric

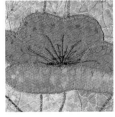

THREE POPPIES

Patricia Archibald
West Lothian, Scotland
2003
25 × 35" (64 × 87 cm)

At first glance this quilt appears to be relatively simple, but closer examination reveals some delightful details. The three poppies have been applied with reverse appliqué techniques, on a strip-pieced background. Metallic threads and beading are used for the stamens. Chain-stitch embroidery echoes the outlines of the flower. The single curved border and red inset strip is a reminder of the sinuous curves and vitality of these fragile flowers.

can be dip-dyed in small pots of color. Watercolor pencils, crayons and pastels are also ideal for highlighting details on petals and leaves and for adding definition or blending color changes at seams.

For many contemporary quiltmakers, one of the prime reasons for dyeing, painting, and screen-printing their own cloth is the element of chance that is an integral part of the process. No two lengths of fabric will be the same. Even if the same dye is used, there will be minor differences in the depth of color, the mottling or the texture. Such fabrics are ideal when interpreting blooms, since few flower heads have a flat surface of color. Strident parrot tulips, old-fashioned, velvety roses, and sculptural tiger lilies are examples of dazzling color changes.

American quilter Jan Myers-Newbury is well-known for using her own dyed fabrics. She eloquently describes the serendipity that can occur with hand-dyeing or, as she calls it, "the nuances of the dyepot" and how it affects her work:

Whereas earlier I dyed fabrics to impose a design on them, now the fabrics themselves have a strong voice and in large part determine the finished work.

This point of view is an approach shared by many. German quilter Elsbeth Nusser-Lampe is typical of quilt artists for whom the unpredictable results of a dyed fabric suggest the subject matter of the quilt. Her quilt *Changing Dandelion* (page 133) is an example of serendipity leading to a finished quilt.

Quilters new to hand-dyeing should not feel obliged to use only one-of-a-kind fabrics in their quilts. Hand-dyed and painted materials also work well with commercial prints. They add an unpredictable edge to the quilt, particularly when used in pieced block quilts. This ensures that no two blocks are identical. Commercially manufactured batiked and marbled materials can also be successfully used for petals and leaves and are now available world-wide in collections of more than 100 colors.

IN LOVE WITH IRISES

Emilie M Belak
British Columbia, Canada
1996
63½ × 49½"
(161 × 126 cm)

The power of this embroidered and appliquéd quilt is even more impressive when you consider the scale. Each flower is about 30 inches (76 cm) tall. Photographs from Emilie's own garden were used to create the design. Emilie's admiration for the work of artist Georgia O'Keefe is apparent in the realism she has created through stitching. The strongly contrasting, abstract background fabric was created by Caryl Bryer Fallert.

Finally, remember that in past years quilters did not have the luxury of local quilt shops and Internet shopping. If they ran out of one color or pattern, they substituted another in the remaining blocks and borders. Such forced adaptations often led to better quilts and prevented beautifully sewn quilts from appearing too perfect and soulless.

THREE-DIMENSIONAL QUILTS

Adding a third dimension to the flat surface of a quilt is another option for some quilters. Folded and ruched patchwork techniques can be traditional, such as Prairie Points (patches of fabric folded to form enclosed triangles) or Yo-Yo patches (material circles that are gathered by a running stitch around

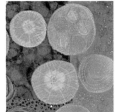

SPRING

Elsbeth Nusser-Lampe
Freiburg, Germany
2000
51 × 51"
(130 × 130 cm)

The vibrant colors in this quilt are a joyful evocation of bright spring bulbs and the sharp greens of new plant shoots and leaves. The patchwork background is pieced from various sizes of sap green rectangles, all cleverly slotted together. The circular appliqué motifs are randomly scattered across the surface, and their shapes are echoed by the free machine quilting. A pieced binding incorporates many of the green shades used in the quilt.

the edge). Cathedral Window and Secret Garden (squares folded and refolded to make segment-type patches) are other alternatives for abstract floral designs. All these patches can be used to suggest petals, leaves, or complete flowers. In contemporary quilts, extra texture can be added in areas requiring extra definition. Folded fabric or piping can be inserted in seams to suggest the veins of a leaf, or tucks can be taken in the fabric before a motif is applied. If you are doing the latter, remember that you need to cut larger motifs to allow for the tucks. Try experimenting with different pieces of scrap fabric first so you can determine how much extra is needed and the width and distance of the tucks.

Another possibility for textured quilts is a technique known as fabric snippets, pioneered by American quilter Cindy Walter. For this particular method, tiny, irregular pieces of fabric are bonded onto a foundation material using a fusible adhesive (bonding agent). The process is ideal for creating a rich, colorful, and extremely tactile pictorial quilt in which the many colored and patterned fabrics merge to form a vibrant whole. If the quilter wishes, this can be embellished further with free machine stitching or embroidery.

ROSE COTTAGE

Wendy Lawson

London, England

1998

39 × 49"

(99 × 124 cm)

This floral quilt is made from flower petals, leaves, and grasses laminated onto fabric. Wendy developed this innovative technique which is heavily quilted and mounted on stiff board.

A more advanced way of achieving surface texture is to construct the petals and leaves separately with a double facing (much like a collar on a shirt) and then attach them to the surface of the quilt. Emilie Belak used this method for her quilts shown on pages 125 and 128. Wanting the petals at the front of the flowers to be three-dimensional, Emilie painted and stitched both sides of each loose petal. Machine embroidery was then added to give depth to the many hues and shades in each petal. The edges were surrounded in satin stitch for added support.

EMBROIDERY ON QUILTS

Two types of quilts in this book feature embroidery.

Known as Jacobean-style quilts and crazy quilts, both have been sewn for several hundred years. Crazy quilts use an appliqué style to combine irregularly shaped patches on a backing fabric. Particularly popular during the nineteenth century when lavish interior decoration was the norm, crazy quilts were used as decorative throws and piano or table covers. The crazy patches were sewn in a wide variety of fabrics, including silks, satins, grosgrain ribbons, cigarette silks, and velvets.

All the seams were covered in hand embroidery, usually in a contrasting color for maximum impact. The crazy quilt shown on page 138 has many lifelike flowers embroidered at the center of the patches. Ribbon flowers form

WISTERIA LE DEUXIEME

Yvonne Porcella

California, USA

1995

42 × 36"

(107 × 90 cm)

This is one of a series of quilts and wearable art incorporating Yvonne's hand-painted silk. The acrylic based paint is diluted in water to avoid stiffening the fabric, the resulting colors are gentle pastels, a contrast to her brightly colored quilts (page 34). The silks are colored first, and the quilts are then designed to suit the delicately colored one-of-a-kind fabrics. This quilt, inspired by Monet's paintings of wisteria, has burnt-edge appliqué and hand quilting.

a vine in the border. Crazy quilts represent the "more is better" philosophy. One embellished block may look excessive when viewed as a solitary square. However, when the blocks are combined the final effect is of a richly textured, elaborate quilt.

"Jacobean-style" is a loose term used to describe quilts with a distinct appearance reminiscent of early seventeenth-century costume embroidery. The designs often use entwining stems sewn in braid stitch. Within the twisting stems are large blooms, such as white roses, thistles, and pansies. Gold cord and beading are part of the decoration.

Another embroidery term, crewel work, describes the way embroidery is used with fine

ANGELICA GIGAS
Angela Chisholm
Midlothian, Scotland
2002
43½ × 31"
(110 × 77 cm)

This richly textured quilt is best viewed close up to fully appreciate the fine detail. The design was first painted on silk organza and then placed on felt. Layers of silk were built up until the desired strength of colors was achieved. The flowers and leaves were then heavily machine embroidered. Finally, a layer of batting was added, and the quilt was finished with machine quilting.

worsted yarn, usually on a linen ground. Several quilts featured, such as *Stomacher* (page 137), *Embroidered Quilt* (page 134), and *Little Brown Bird* (page 27) show influences of this style of embroidery.

In recent years, embroidery has been increasingly used on quilts, as shown by *In Praise of Poppies* (page 125) and *Angelica Gigas* (page 132 and 132). This can take the form of freestyle hand or machine stitching for a subtle blending of colors or more traditional pictorial embroidery for flowers. The latter is shown to great effect in Margarete

Heinisch's quilt *Sleeping in my Heart* (page 136). It incorporates fragments of an old dress belonging to her mother, reinterpreted as a shawl. Stunning new embroidery is used on a traditional folkloric apron.

Beading can suggest pollen and stamen heads, and buttons make interesting flower or seed heads. Obviously, the borders between embroidery, quiltmaking and textiles have blurred as the two textile art crafts merge. For many artists whose work includes several techniques, rigid classification is deemed unimportant. They are comfortable combining old and new techniques from many areas of textiles.

MODERN TECHNIQUES

Today's quilters are free to incorporate new and innovative techniques and materials in their projects. As quilts become less functional, alternatives to fabric such as paper and plastic are also used. British quilter Gillian Travis makes her own surfaces for stitching from silk cocoon strippings and felt made from merino wool tops. Although not fabrics as such, her pieces are sandwiched with padding like a traditional three-layer quilt and feature decorative stitching. To make her work look old, Gillian distresses the fabric by spilling coffee onto the quilt after she has painted and stitched the design.

Laminating is another method of permanently securing non textile items such as leaves, feathers, and flower petals onto a fabric base. The finished laminated quilt makes an

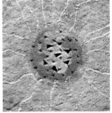

CHANGING DANDELION
Elsbeth Nusser-Lampe
Freiburg, Germany
2002
51 × 51"
(130 × 130 cm)

This triptych of panels celebrates the life of the dandelion—from seed to flower and back again to wind-blown seed. Each panel has a hand-dyed cotton background, featuring machine embroidery on a water-soluble fabric or appliqué on voile. The quilt was theme winner of Husqvarna Viking's "Feel Free" competition, 2002.

interesting wall hanging. British quilt artist Pauline Burbidge has been working with this technique for some years. Her *Color Study* quilts use leaves, grasses, and flower petals that she collected and pressed over the seasons. Pauline uses the laminating plastic to sandwich the natural objects onto a fabric background. Then the blocks are machine stitched and combined to form the whole quilt. Despite the rigidity of the quilt surface, Pauline can hand-quilt her pieces using a traditional large floor frame and large stitches (about ¾ inch [2 cm] in length).

Pauline is best known for the strikingly modern graphic quilts she has been sewing professionally for more than 20 years. By collecting natural objects for a year before starting her floral quilts, she acknowledges that the task increased her appreciation for the colors in nature:

EMBROIDERED QUILT

Maker unknown
England
1700–1725
76 × 62"
(193 × 157 cm)

This fine hand-embroidered quilt is one of the earliest documented quilts in England. Made of linen and silk, the surface is covered in a delicate trellis of flowering branches that surround the central monogram.
Bowes Museum

ELIZABETHAN DESIGN REVISITED I

Gillian Travis
West Yorkshire, England
2002
53 × 32"
(135 × 81 cm)

Although made three centuries after the quilt shown opposite, Gillian's quilt was actually based on even earlier source material. She used a seventeenth-century embroidered jacket and woodcut patterns from early herb books. The base of the quilt is silk paper with a batting of merino wool felt. Acrylic paint was used for the flowers, which have a distressed feel. The meandering gold cord was couched in place and the lace border was embroidered on dissolvable fabric.

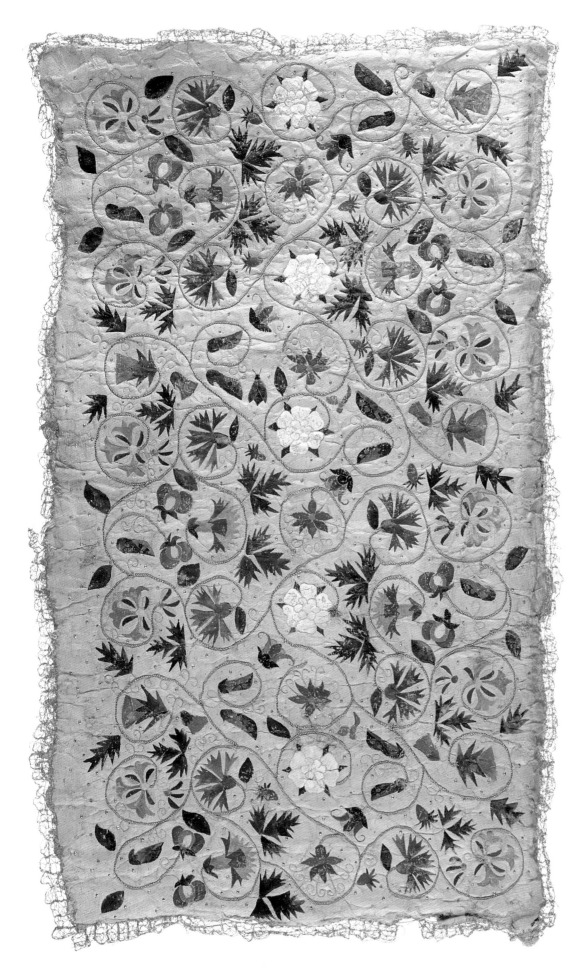

I worked through the seasons collecting color. Without being aware of it, I was observing and recording color that was all around me. The experience heightened my color sensitivity.

Another technique used to create firm, one-of-a-kind fabrics is to transfer photo images onto fabric. In this case, images of flowers and foliage can be copied from photographs onto fabrics using a transfer liquid and a photocopy

SLEEPING IN MY HEART

Margarete Heinisch
California, USA
2002
48 × 70"
(122 × 178 cm)

This quilt recalls deep personal memories. Margarete was given a dress by her mother and was told to, "do something with it." Fifty years later, the dress, which has embroidery typical of Czechoslavakia (now the Czech Republic), has become a shawl in a quilt portrait that honors her mother and Margarete's heritage. The quilt was awarded second place for pictorial quilts in Quilts, A World of Beauty, USA, 2002.

machine. The reverse printed image can then be cut for resewing and embellishment to achieve a photo-realism style of quilt.

Floral quilts have been a source of joy and inspiration for hundreds of thousands of quilters over the centuries. Long may these quilts continue to flourish and delight.

STOMACHER
Gillian Travis
West Yorkshire, England
2001
16 × 12" (40 × 30 cm)

This jewel of textile art is mounted on a base that befits a precious historical fragment in a museum. Despite its small size, it features a great deal of details: tucked silk paper, machine embroidery on the scrim surface, and lacing with gold cord in the manner of old corsets. The wide variety of flowers, such as daffodils and columbines, is typical of embroidered designs from sixteenth- and seventeenth-century fashions.

TECHNIQUE
CRAZY PATCHWORK AND EMBROIDERY
INSPIRED BY THE QUILT: CRAZY QUILT

CRAZY QUILT

Maker unknown, possibly Ohio, USA

c. 1890

64 × 68" (163 × 173 cm)

At the center of this luxurious silk quilt is an embroidered sunflower, a symbol of adoration. Randomly pieced patches are covered in large-scale embroidery stitches. The larger patches are embellished with embroidered fuchsias, pansies, daisies, and rosebuds. Although weighty with embroidery, the quilt is not actually quilted with a batting (wadding). The outer silk border contains a wild rose vine and scalloped lace edging. University of Nebraska-Lincoln

In crazy patchwork, the more embellishment the better. This decorative technique is ideal for small cushions or pillows if you do not wish to tackle a large quilt. For a sumptuous effect, you need to collect luxurious fabrics—even tiny scraps will do. Start from one corner, since it is easiest to then work on the block from three angles. The patches must extend beyond the drawn outline. Continue with various shapes and fabrics until the whole area is covered.

MATERIALS FOR ONE BLOCK

- Background square of lightweight cotton
- Scraps of velvet, silk, and satin
- Pencil
- Basting thread
- Embroidery threads
- Needle

1 Use a rotary square to make a template and draw an outline of the area to be covered.

2 Starting in a corner, baste (tack) a patch onto the background. Place the second patch either under or over the first, making sure that raw edges are covered. When happy with the design, baste (tack) through the layers. Continue with various shapes and fabrics, covering the whole area.

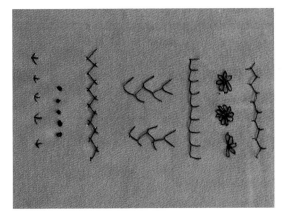

3 Secure the patches with hand embroidery. Make sure you sew through all the layers including the background. Embroider flowers in the larger patches. Remove all basting threads.

EMBROIDERY STIITCHES (from left to right)

Fly stitch
French knot – mostly used in clusters for floral centers
Herringbone stitch
Feather stitch
Blanket stitch
Lazy-daisy stitch and half flower
Open Cretan stitch

TECHNIQUE
PAINTING AND COUCHING
INSPIRED BY THE QUILT: DENIM QUILT

DENIM QUILT

Gillian Travis, West Yorkshire, England, 2003

39 × 59" (100 × 150 cm)

Gillian had previously sewn several pieces as a result of her research into Elizabethan flowers (pages 135 and 137). This quilt incorporates the same style of flower, but this time it is given a 1960s makeover as a quilt deliberately designed to have rough and frayed edges. The flowers were painted onto the sewn patches. Then, in imitation of the gold embroidery and lace edging, thread stems were couched in a meandering pattern across the quilt surface, and a looped binding was attached to the edge.

This quilt proves that contemporary projects, like the feedsack quilts of the 1930s and Victorian silk crazy quilts, can make use of whatever fabrics are available. In this case, many shades of blue denim are patched together. All parts of the jeans have been used, including zippers, metal buttons, pockets, fabric, and leather labels. Denim is a particularly tough and hard-wearing material, so the floral decoration is similarly striking. Fabric paints are used to paint large, bold flowers onto patches, which are then decorated with machine stitching and hand made couched yarns.

MATERIALS FOR ONE BLOCK

- One pair of old blue jeans
- 8 × 8" (20 × 20 cm) light iron-on interfacing
- 4 × 4" (10 × 10 cm) plastic template
- Blue pen
- Paper and fabric scissors
- Pins
- Sewing machine with free machining facility and cording foot
- 100/16 sewing machine needle or a denim needle
- Blue thread
- Stiff card stock for making flower template
- Opaque fabric paint in red, yellow, and green
- Paint brush
- Jeans top stitching threads in red and green
- Orange hand stitching thread
- Needles
- Short lengths of assorted blue threads or wools

1 Make a 4 × 4" (10 × 10 cm) template using transparent plastic. Place the template on the right side of the denim and draw around it carefully with a blue pen. The transparent template allows you to choose an interesting piece of denim. (Avoid large metal rivets, which are impossible to stitch over.) Cut three more denim squares using different parts of the blue jeans.

2 Place the interfacing, adhesive side up, on the work surface. Pin the denim pieces, right sides up, over the interfacing, abutting the edges.

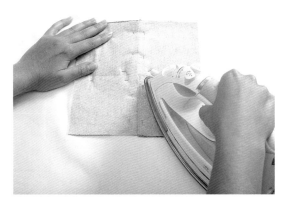

3 Press carefully. Remove the pins.

4 Machine stitch the patches on the right side using a feather stitch and blue thread. Make sure that the stitching is accurately placed to join the pieces.

5 Trace the flower pattern from the template on page 151, and cut out from stiff paper. Place the template on the denim, and draw around it using a blue ballpoint pen.

6 Paint the flower with opaque red and green fabric paint. Add shading to the flower by using yellow paint. Two coats of paint may be needed to give the vibrancy required.

7 Free machine stitch around the edge of the painted flower, using a jeans top stitching thread. It is not necessary to stitch the flower shape precisely.

8 Hand stitch large line stitches onto the flower as shown, using the orange thread.

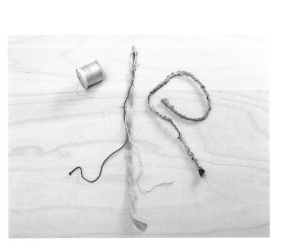

9 Make a blue cord using ¼" (7 mm) strips of denim and other blue threads. A cording foot allows you to push the fabric and threads through the hole while zigzagging over the threads. This produces a rounded cord. Alternatively, you can make a twisted cord by hand.

10 Couch the cord in place by hand as shown on the finished block.

TEMPLATES

All of the following templates are shown at 100%. Please refer to the projects for the correction dimensions of the fabric required for each piece.

PAGE 46

PAGE 48

PAGE 51

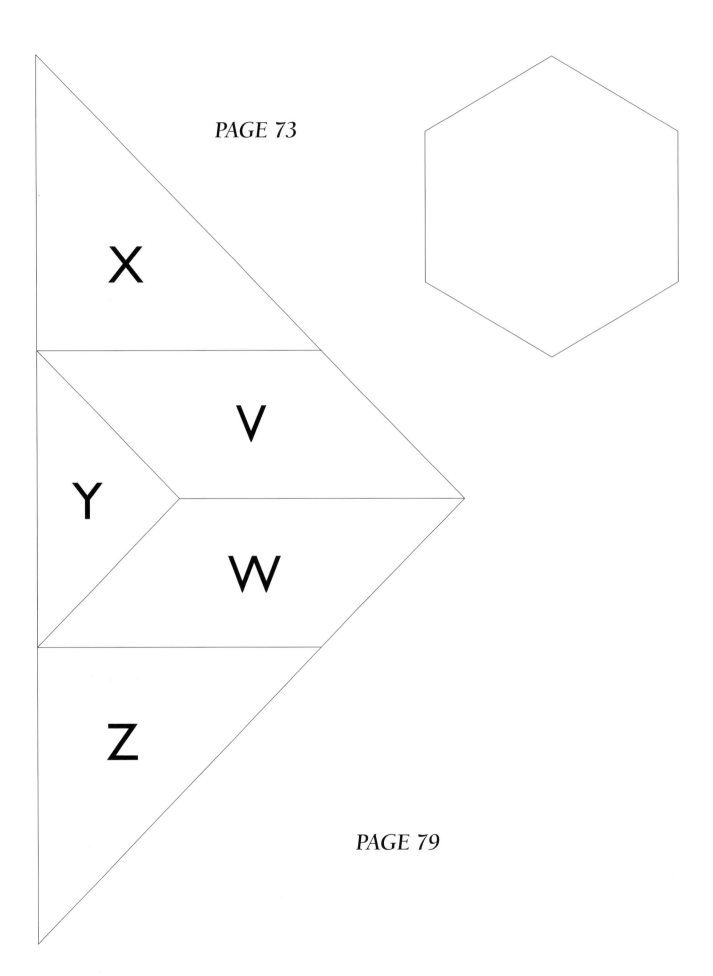

PAGE 73

X

V

Y

W

Z

PAGE 79

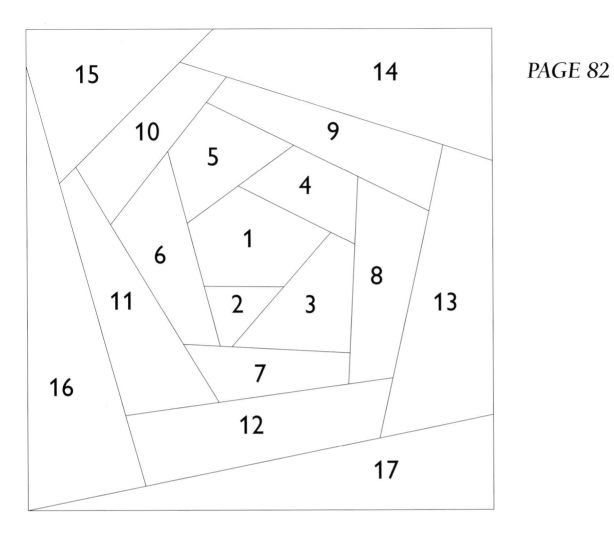

PAGE 82

PAGE 100

PAGE 98

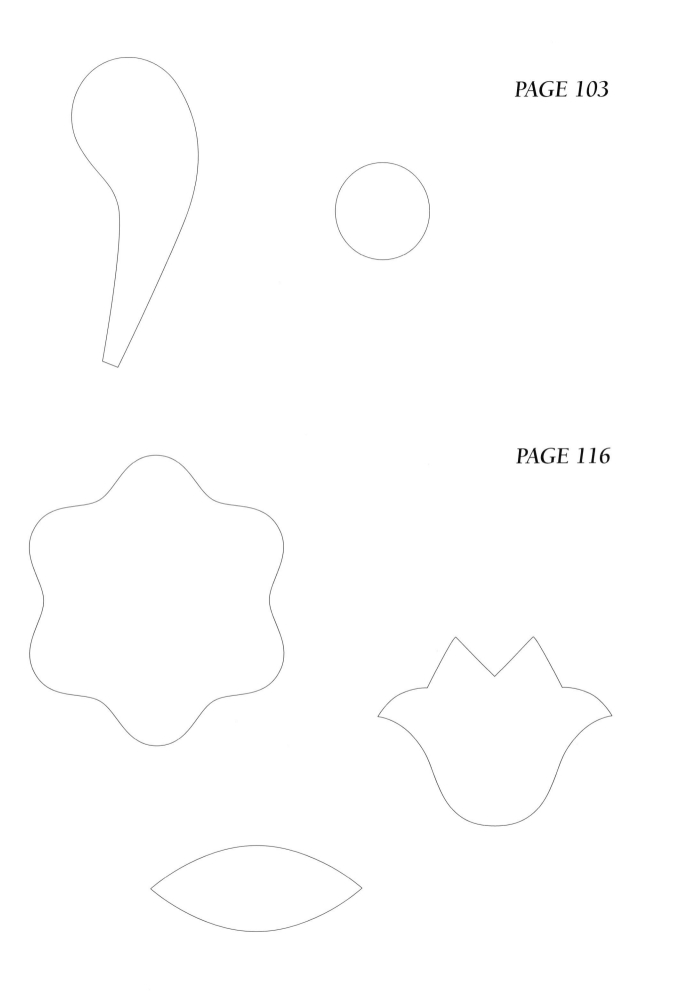

PAGE 103

PAGE 116

PAGE 119

PAGE 140

UK COUNTIES

These flowers were voted for by the general public on a Internet poll in 2003 sponsored by Laura Ashley for the Plantlife charity. Note that the county names used are the old county divisions not the current postal counties and metropolitan districts.

Aberdeenshire *Bearberry, Harebell*

Anglesey *Spotted Rock-Rose, Spring Squill*

Angus *Alpine Blue-Sow-Thistle, Alpine Catchfly*

Antrim *Bog Myrtle (Sweet Gale), Harebell*

Argyllshire *Yellow Oxytropis, Foxglove*

Armagh *Bog Rosemary, Cowbane*

Ayrshire *Oysterplant, Green-winged Orchid*

Banffshire *Dark Red, Grass of Parnassus*

Bedfordshire *Pasqueflower, Bee Orchid*

Belfast *Common Poppy, Gorse*

Berkshire Summer Snowflake *(Loddon Lily), Bee Orchid*

Berwickshire *Rock Rose, Roseroot*

Birmingham *Broad-leaved Willowherb, Foxglove*

Brecknockshire *Cuckooflower (Lady's Smock), Ivy-leaved Bellflower*

Bristol *Primrose, Maltese-Cross (Flower of Bristol)*

Buckinghamshire *Chiltern Gentian, Bee Orchid*

Buteshire *Thrift, Lady's Mantle*

Caernarvonshire *Snowdon Lily, Welsh Poppy*

Caithness *Scots Primrose, Bog Asphodel*

Cambridgeshire *Pasqueflower, Cowslip*

Cardiff *Daffodil (wild), Dune Gentian*

Cardiganshire *Bog Rosemary, Daffodil (wild)*

Carmarthenshire *Whorled Caraway, Daffodil (wild)*

Cheshire *Cuckooflower (lady's smock), Cowbane*

Clackmannanshire *Opposite-leaved Golden Saxifrage, Dog's Mercury*

Cornwall *Cornish Heath, Primrose*

Cromartyshire *Spring Cinquefoil, Pyramidal Bugle*

Cumberland *Daffodil (wild), Grass of Parnassus*

Denbighshire *Limestone Woundwort, Western Gorse*

Derbyshire *Jacob's Ladder, Alpine Currant*

Derry *Bog Rosemary, Purple Saxifrage*

Devon *Primrose, Sweet Violet*

Dorset *Dorset Heath, Early Spider Orchid*

Down *Spring Squill, Irish Lady's Tresses*

Dumfriesshire *Harebell (Scottish Bluebell), Sweet Cicely*

Dunbartonshire *Harebell (Scottish Bluebell), Lesser Water Plantain*

Durham *Spring Gentian, Bird's-eye Primrose*

East Lothian *Cowslip, Viper's Bugloss*

Edinburgh *Sticky Catchfly, Harebell*

Essex *Bird's Foot Trefoil, Common Poppy*

Fermanagh *Marsh Violet, Globeflower*

Fife *Coralroot Orchid, Cowberry (Red Whortleberry)*

Flintshire *Bell Heather, Welsh Groundsel*

Glamorgan *Dandelion, Yellow Whitlowgrass*

Glasgow *Broad-leaved Helleborine, Broom*

Gloucestershire *Daffodil (wild), Adder's-tongue Spearwort*

Hampshire *Dog Rose, Bell Heather*

Herefordshire *Mistletoe, Common Dog-violet*

Hertfordshire *Pasqueflower, Cowslip*

Huntingdonshire *Common Poppy, Water Violet*

Inverness-shire *Twinflower, Blue Heath*

Isle of Man *Fuchsia, Isle of Man Cabbage*

Isle of Wight *Bastard Balm, Pyramidal Orchid*

Isles of Scilly *Thrift, Red Campion*

Kent *Hop, Lady Orchid*

Kincardineshire *Clustered Bellflower, Melancholy Thistle*

Kinross-shire *Holy Grass, Monk's Rhubarb*

Kirkcudbrightshire *Bog Rosemary, Harebell (Scottish Bluebell)*

Lanarkshire *Harebell (Scottish Bluebell), Dune Helleborine*

Lancashire *Red Rose, Bee Orchida*

Leeds *Tufted Vetch, Bilberry*

Leicestershire *Foxglove, Arrowhead*

Lincolnshire *Adder's-tongue (Fern), Common Dog-violet*

Liverpool *Daffodil (wild), Sea Holly*

London *Rosebay Willowherb, London Rocket*
Manchester *Common Cotton Grass, Rosebay Willowherb*
Merioneth *Welsh Poppy, Touch-me-not Balsam*
Middlesex *Yellow Iris, Wood Anemone*
Midlothian *Few-flowered Leek, Sticky Catchfly*
Monmouthshire *Daffodil (wild), Foxglove*
Montgomeryshire *Floating Water Plantain, Spiked Speedwell*
Morayshire *Creeping Lady's-tresses, One-flowered Wintergreen (St Olaf's Candlestick)*
Nairnshire *Chickweed Wintergreen, Stone Bramble*
Newcastle-upon-Tyne *Butterbur, Monkeyflower*
Norfolk *Common Poppy, Alexanders*
Northamptonshire *Dog Rose, Cowslip*
Northumberland *Bloody Crane's-bill, Alpine Cinquefoil*
Nottingham *Nottingham Catchfly, Meadow Crane's-bill*
Nottinghamshire *Autumn Crocus, Sweet Violet*
Orkney *Scots Primrose, Alpine Bearberry*
Oxfordshire *Fritillary, Meadow Clary*
Peeblesshire *Cloudberry, Gorse*
Pembrokeshire *Tenby Daffodil, Thrift*
Perthshire *Alpine Gentian, Yellow Saxifrage*
Radnorshire *Early Star of Bethlehem, Western Gorse*
Renfrewshire *Bogbean, Harebell (Scottish Bluebell)*
Ross-shire *Bog Asphodel, Pale Butterwort*
Roxburghshire *Maiden Pink, Great Burnet*
Rutland *Clustered Bellflower, Cowslip*
Selkirkshire *Mountain Pansy, Yellow Star of Bethlehem*
Sheffield *Betony, Wood Crane's-bill*
Shetland *Red Campion, Shetland Mouse Ear*
Shropshire *Honeysuckle, Round-leaved Sundew*
Somerset *Cheddar Pink. Cowslip*
Staffordshire *Cuckooflower (Lady's Smock), Heather*
Stirlingshire *Sweet Cicely, Scottish Dock*
Suffolk *Bee Orchid, Oxlip*
Surrey *Cowslip, Dog Rose*
Sussex *Round-headed Rampion, Bird's-foot Trefoil*
Sutherland *Grass of Parnassus, Round-leaved Sundew*

Tyrone *Corn Marigold, Bog Rosemary*
Warwickshire *Honeysuckle, Dog Rose*
West Lothian *Common Spotted Orchid, Leopard's Bane*
Western Isles *Hebridean Spotted Orchid, Corn Marigold*
Westmoreland *Daffodil (wild), Alpine Forget-me-not*
Wigtownshire *Yellow Iris, Oysterplant*
Wiltshire *Wiltshire Fritillary, Burnt Orchid*
Worcestershire *Mistletoe, Cowslip*
Yorkshire *Harebell, Baneberry*

US STATE FLOWERS

The Latin name is shown in brackets together with the year of adoption by the state.

Alabama *Camellia (Camellia japonica L.) 1999*
Alaska *Wild Native Forget-Me-Not (Myosotis alpestris) 1917*
Arizona *Saguaro Cactus (Cereus giganteus) 1931*
Arkansas *Apple Blossom (Pyrus coronaria) 1901*
California *Golden Poppy (Eschscholtzia californica) 1903*
Colorado *White and Lavender Columbine (Aquilegia caerules) 1899*
Connecticut *Mountain Laurel (Kalmia latifolia) 1907*
Delaware *Peach Blossom (Prunus persica) 1895*
Florida *Orange Blossom (Citrus sinensis) 1909*
Georgia *Cherokee Rose (Rosa laevigata) 1916*
Hawaii *Native Yellow Hibiscus (Hibiscus brackenridgei A. Gray) 1988*
Idaho *Syringa (Philadelphus lewisii) 1931*
Illinois *Native Violet (Viola sororia) 1908*
Indiana *Peony (Paeonie) 1957*
Iowa *Wild Rose (Rosa Pratincola) 1897*
Kansas *Common Sunflower (Helianthus annuus) 1903*
Kentucky *Goldenrod (Solidago spp.) 1926*
Louisiana *Magnolia (Magnolia graniflora) 1900*
Maine *White Pine Cone and Tassel (Pinus strobus, linnaeus) 1895*

Maryland *Black-Eyed Susan (Rudbeckia hirta)
1918*

Massachusetts *Mayflower (Epigaea regens)
1918*

Michigan *Apple Blossom (Pyrus coronaria)
1897*

Minnesota *Pink and White Lady's Slipper
(Cypripedium reginae) 1893*

Mississippi *Magnolia (Magnolia grandiflora)
1952*

Missouri *Hawthorn (Crataegus) 1923*

Montana *Bitterroot (Lewisia rediviva) 1895*

Nebraska *Goldenrod (Solidago serotina) 1895*

Nevada *Sage Brush (Artemisia tridentata or
trifida) 1967*

New Hampshire *Purple Lilac (Syringa vulgaris)
1919*

New Jersey *Purple Violet (Viola sororia) 1913*

New Mexico *Yucca Flower (Yucca glauca)
1927*

New York *Rose (Rosa) 1955*

North Carolina *Dogwood (Cornus florida)
1941*

North Dakota *Wild Prairie Rose (Rosa
setigera) 1907*

Ohio *Scarlet Carnation (Trillium grandiflorum)
1904*

Oklahoma *Mistletoe (Phoradendron serotinum)
1893*

Oregon *Oregon Grape (Berberis aquifolium)
1899*

Pennsylvania *Wild Mountain Laurel (Kalmia
latifolia) 1933*

Rhode Island *Violet (Viola Palmata) 1968*

South Carolina *Carolina or Yellow Jessamine
(Gelsemium sempervirens) 1924*

South Dakota *Pasque, May Day Flower
(Pulsatilla hirsutissima) 1903*

Tennessee *Iris (genus Iridaceae) 1933*

Texas *Bluebonnet (Lupinus subcarnosus)
(Lupinus texensis) 1901*

Utah *Sego Lily (Calochortus nuttallii) 1911*

Vermont *Red Clover (Trifolium pratense) 1894*

Virginia *American Dogwood (Cornus florida)
1918*

Washington *7Coast Rhododendron
(Rhododendron macrophyllum) 1892*

West Virginia *Big Laurel (Rhododendron
Maximum) 1903*

Wisconsin *Wood Violet (Viola papilionacea)
1949*

Wyoming *Indian Paint Brush (Castilleja
linariaefolia) 1917*

*Note: In Illinois, Missouri, and Texas there are
several species that fit the legislated name of
the state flower.*

AUSTRALIAN STATES

As well as having individual flowers for each
of the seven states, Australia considers the
Golden Wattle (Acacia pycantha), to be its
national flower. The state flowers are all
species native only to Australia.

New South Wales *Warratah (Telopea
speciosissima) 1962 although roses are
featured on the capital Sydney's coat of arms*

Northern Territory *Sturt's Desert Rose
(Gossypium sturtianum) 1964*

Queensland *Cooktown Orchid (Denrobium
bigibbum) 1959*

South Australia *Sturt's Desert Pea (Clianthus
formosus) 1961*

Tasmania *Tasmanian Blue Gum (Eucalyptus
globulus) 1962*

Victoria *Common Heath, Pink Heath (Epacris
impressa) 1958*

Western Australia *Red and Green Kangaroo
Paw, Mangle's Kangaroo Paw (Anigozanthos
manglesii) 1960*

FURTHER READING

1000 Great Quilt Blocks
Maggi McCormick
Collins & Brown, 2003

101 Patchwork Patterns
Ruby McKim
Dover Publications, 1962

A Flowering of Quilts
Patricia Cox Crews
University of Nebraska, 2001

American Quilt Classics
Patricia Cox
Collins & Brown, 2001

Art & Inspirations
Yvonne Porcella
C&T Publishing, 1998

*Colourwash Quilts: A Personal Approach to
    Design and Techniques*
Deirdre Amsden
Martingale, 1994

Dutch Flower Pots
Anja Townrow
American Quilter's Society, 2000

Enchanted Views
Dilys Fronks
C&T Publishing, 2002

*Enduring Grace - Quilts from the Shelburne
    Museum Collection*
Celia Y Oliver
C&T Publishing, 1997

Fabric Collage Quilts
Joanne Goldstein
Martingale, 1999

Little Brown Bird
Margaret Docherty
American Quilter's Society, 1999

Northern Comfort - New England's Early Quilts
Lynne Z Bassett and Jack Larkin
Rutledge Hill Press, 1998

Pieced Flowers
Ruth B McDowell
C&T Publishing, 2000

Quilts in Bloom exhibition catalogue
Diane Leone
Quilts in Bloom, 1999

Quilts: The American Story
Susan Jenkins and Linda Seward
Harper Collins, 1991

Redwork Romance
Alex Anderson
C&T Publishing, 2002

Roses (Pierre Joseph Redouté)
PA Hine and B Schulz
Taschen, 1999

Squaredance
Martha Thompson
That Patchwork Place, 1995

The Hawaiian Quilt - A Spiritual Experience
Poakalani and John Serrao
Mutual Publishing, 1997

The New England Quilt Museum Quilts
Jennifer Gilbert
C&T Publishing, 1999

The Quilted Garden
Jane Sassaman
C&T Publishing, 2000

The Twentieth Century's Best American Quilts
Editor Mary Leman Austin
Primedia, 1999

MUSEUM COLLECTIONS

Not all museums have their quilt collections on permanent display, so telephone before making a special journey.

Australia
Powerhouse Museum
500 Harris Street, Ultimo, Sydney 2000
tel 02 9217 0111
www.phm.gov.au

United Kingdom
American Museum in Britain
Claverton Manor, Bath BA2 7BD
tel 01225 460503
www.americanmuseum.org

Bowes Museum
Castle Barnard, Co Durham DL12 8NP
tel 01833 690606
www.bowesmuseum.org.uk

Museum of Welsh Life
St Fagans, Cardiff CF5 6XB
tel 029 2057 3500
www.nmgw.ac.uk

North of England Open Air Museum
Beamish, County Durham DH9 0RG
tel 01207 231811
www.beamish.org.uk

Ulster Folk and Transport Museum
Cultra, Holywood, Belfast, County Down
BT18 0EU
tel 028 90 428428
www.nidex.com/uftm

USA
Museum of the American Quilter's Society
215 Jefferson Street
Paducah, Kentucky 42001
tel 502 442 8856
www.quiltmuseum.org

New England Quilt Museum
18 Shattuck Street, Lowell,
Massachusetts 01852
tel 978 452 4207
www.nequiltmuseum.org

People's Place Quilt Museum
Main Street, Intercourse, Philadelphia 17534
tel 717 768 7101
www.ppquiltmuseum.com

Shelburne Museum
5555 Shelburne Road, Shelburne, Vermont
tel 802 985 3346
www.shelburnemuseum.org

International Quilt Study Center
University of Nebraska-Lincoln
1155 Q Street, Hewitt Place, Lincoln,
Nebraska
tel 402 472 6301
http://quiltstudy.unl.edu

ORGANIZATIONS AND EXHIBITIONS

American Quilter's Society,
PO Box 3290, Paducah, KY 42002-3290, USA
tel +1 270 898 7903
www.AQSquilt.com
Society open to members internationally organizing annual expositions in Paducah and Nashville

Carrefour Européen du Patchwork
tel +33 3 89 58 80 50
www.patchwork-europe.com
Annual multi-venue exhibition and workshops in Alsace, France organized by the l'Office du Tourisme du Val d'Argent

European Quilt Championships
tel +31 40 221 2184
www.quilt@pi.be

Organizers of an annual exhibition in the Netherlands

International Machine Quilters' Association
tel +1 870 236 6587
www.imqa.org
Organizers of the annual Machine Quilters' Showcase exhibition for long arm quilting in Springfield, Illinois

Mancuso Show Management
PO Box 667, New Hope, PA 18938, USA
tel +1 215 862 5828
www.quiltfest.com
Organizers of the Mid Atlantic Quilt Festival, Williamsburg Quilt Festival and other large quilt shows

Quilts Inc
7660 Woodway, Suite 550, Houston,
Texas 77063, USA
tel +1 713 781 6864
www.quilts.com
Organizers of the International Quilt Festival held annually in Houston and other cities in the USA, and the biennial Quilt Expo held in Europe and other competitive and juried exhibitions. The International Quilt Association is at the same address

The Appliqué Society
PO Box 89, Sequim, WA 98382-0089, USA
tel +1 800 597 9827
www.theappliquesociety.org
International society open to all those interested in appliqué. Organises annual seminars, local membership groups in the US.

The Quilters' Guild of the British Isles
Room 190, Dean Clough, Halifax HX3 5AX, UK
tel 01422 347669
www.quiltersguild.org.uk
Organization open to quiltmakers in Britain and world-wide. Young quilters' membership also available for those under 18. Resource center with changing exhibitions and library

PHOTOGRAPHY AND PROJECT CREDITS

All photographs by the quiltmakers with the exception of the following:

James Austin 58, 59 (top)
Kathleen Bellesiles 34
Robert Claxton 63
Creative Exhibitions 107
Theresa Fleming 108
Steve Gold 13
Charles R. Lynch 7, 27
Michael Motron 115, 79
Peter Naylor 100, 20
Karen Perrine 128
Brian Pollard 67
Sharon Risedorph 31, 131
David Stansbury 26
Carina Woolrich 125
Ben/New Medium.co.nz 35

Jonathan Farmer
Photography of quilts: 14, 15, 17, 19, 36, 37, 38, 39, 40, 41 (top), 44, 45, 59 (bottom), 60 (bottom), 61, 62, 64, 65 (top), 66 (bottom), 70, 77, 82, 87, 88 (all), 92, 93, 95 (all), 111, 112, 127, 130, 132, 135, 137, 140
Photography of projects: 46, 48, 51, 73, 97

Thomas Skovsende
Photography of projects: 76, 79, 82, 100, 103, 116, 119, 138, 140

Quilting projects supplied by the following people:

Marion Haslam 46, 48, 51, 73
Jinny Jarry 76
Melyn Robinson 79, 82, 103, 116
Sue Harmsworth 97, 138
Christine Thomas 100
Christine Dobson 119
Gillian Travis 140

INDEX

Page numbers in *italics* refer to quilt illustrations & captions. Page numbers in **bold** refer to projects & project templates. Quilt names appear in *italics*.

SOURCES

UK

Busy Bees
The Craft Units, Tredegar
House, Newport, South Wales
NP10 9TW
tel 01633 810801

Creative Grids
(mail order only)
Unit 28, Swannington Road,
Broughton, Astley, Leicester
LE9 6TU
tel 01455 286787
www.creativegrids.com

Creative Quilting
32 Bridge Road, East Molesey,
Surrey KT8 9HA
tel 020 8941 7075
www.creativequilting.co.uk

Inca
10 Duke Street, Princes
Risborough, Bucks
HP27 0AT
tel 01844 343343
www.incastudio.com

Kaleidoscope Books
(mail order only)
5 Pendicle Road, Bearsden,
Glasgow G61 1PU
tel 0141 942 8511
special bookseller for quilting
books

Quilters Haven

68 High Street, Wickham
Market, Suffolk IP13 0QU
tel 01728 746275
www.quilters-haven.co.uk

Strawberry Fayre
(mail order only)
Chagford, Devon TQ13 8EN
tel 01647 433250
www.strawberryfayre.co.uk

The Cotton Patch
1285 Stratford Road, Hall
Green, Birmingham B28 9AJ
tel 0121 702 2840
www.cottonpatch.co.uk

The Quilt Room
20 West Street, Dorking,
Surrey RH4 1BL
tel 01306 740739
www.quiltroom.co.uk

US

Bear Paw Quilt Co.
117 W North Ave
Flora, IL 62839
tel 618-662-3391
www.bearpawquilting.com

Calico Basket Quilt Shop
4114 198th Street
SW Lynnwood,
WA. 425-774-6446
tel 1-800-720-6446

www.calicobasket.com

Fabric, Thread, & Notions for
Quilters
toll-free 1-888-204-4050
tel 303-838-1733
www.craftconn.com

Hamels Fabrics, Quilting and
Sewing Machines
tel 604-824-4930
toll-free 1-877-77-HAMEL
www.hamelsfabrics.com

Quakertown Quilts
Quakertown Quilts
180 S. Friendswood Dr
Friendswood, TX 77546
U.S.A.
www.quakertownquilts.com

The Stitch-N-Frame Shop
2222 S Frontage Rd, Suite D
Vicksburg, MS 39180
tel 601-634-0243
www.stitch-n-frame.net

The Cotton Shop
401½ West 4th St.
The Dalles, OR 97058
tel 1-541-296-5358
www.thecottonshop.net

Threadart
13529-N Skinner Rd.
Cypress, TX 77429
www.threadart.com

AUSTRALIA

Almond Grove Crafts
Pyap via Loxton
South Australia
tel +61 8 8584 9111

Dyed & Gone to Heaven
23 Fred Street
Lewisham NSW 2049
Australia
tel (02) 9560 7625 or 0414 745
287
info@dyedheaven.com

Gecko Gully
PO Box 1201
Werribee Plaza
Victoria 3030
Australia
tel +61 3 9749 5068
email christine@geckogully.com

M&S Textiles Australian fabrics
1/103 Watsonia Rd,
Watsonia, VIC,
Australia, 3087
tel +61 3 9435 7833
deb@thepatchworkgallery.com.au

Renmark Craft Corner
Shop 5 Lefty's Mall
Fourteenth Street,
Renmark
South Australia 5341
tel +61 8 85 865 856
renmarkcraftcorner@hotmail.com

ACKNOWLEDGEMENTS

Dedicated with love to Mavis and Joe Haslam, the best quilter and quilter's roadie I know.

Many thanks to all the quiltmakers who have generously loaned their quilts for use in this book. Thanks are also due to the quilt-makers who helped to sew projects and to Ann Farmer for consulting on the photo shoot. I am also grateful to the following people and organizations for their assistance and in tracking down quiltmakers as I researched the book, Jayne Hill, Kaleidoscope Books, Gul Laporte, Lions Gate Quilters' Guild, Vicki Mangum of Quilts Inc, New England Quilt Museum, Atsuko Ohta of Quilt Tsushin and The Quilters' Guild of the British Isles.

Many thanks to the team at Collins & Brown for allowing me this opportunity; Kate Kirby who initiated the idea and Emma Baxter and Miranda Sessions who completed the project, and photographer Jonathan Farmer. In particular, Miranda's patience in calmly overseeing this project, as I unexpectedly moved job, home and country in the middle of writing this book, is to be commended!

Finally, thanks to my family for their continuing support and unwavering enthusiasm for all my endeavors.

Marion Haslam